"The sublime becoming even more subtly sublime – here is the gate of all wonders." This statement from the opening chapter of the Daoist classic *Dao De Jing (Tao Te Ching)* shows how the single Chinese character "sublime"[玄] discloses profound depth within. In Zen as well, such expressions abound: "Wading through weeds and inquiring into the sublime is solely for the purpose of seeing your true nature" (Case 47, *Gateless Barrier*). This "sublime" suggests the root-source of all things, the profound truth. It also refers, however, to a black color tinted with vermillion. Perhaps these two colors suggest the first sense we humans have while still in the womb: pitch-black mingled with blood-red.

Similarly, when black is to be used in Japanese painting, a layer of red is first spread on the silk cloth. By painting black over the red, the real black color is revealed. This is true of dying as well: before dying threads or cloth black, they are first dyed red. Isn't this black color, tinged with red, a concrete example of the aforementioned "sublime"?

I cannot help but think of this sublime character when reading Jeff Shore's newly published work *Zen Classics for the Modern World*. Not simply because the work itself is sublime; where it comes from is also sublime. That is, through the author's own mastery of Zen, the primary layer has been laid; then, through painstaking research and insightful study, the second layer has been applied.

There are plenty of books on Zen. Unfortunately most of them are either narrow, self-centered preaching or the result of mere academic study. Compared with these, the present book not only reflects the latest academic studies in Zen literature, but is based on thirty years of exhaustive practice under former Tôfukuji Head Abbot and renowned Zen master Kôyûken Keidô Fukushima. Thus I single out this book as sublime.

It includes translations of the *Ten Oxherding Pictures*, Boshan's *Exhortations*, and *Enjoying the Way*. The *Exhortations* and *Enjoying the Way* are especially valuable for their accuracy as the first full translations in English. Further, we can feel the presence directly in the Dharma Talks of Jeff Shore, given twice a year during retreats throughout Europe and the United States. His unstinting efforts guiding the participants are true traces of his compassionate lifeblood. I strongly recommend this book to readers worldwide.

Sodô Yasunaga, Rinzai Zen master,
Department Chair, International Zen Studies,
Hanazono University, Kyoto

Zen Classics for the Modern World

Translations of Chinese Zen Poems & Prose
with
Contemporary Commentary

Zen Classics for the Modern World

Translations of Chinese Zen Poems & Prose
with
Contemporary Commentary

Jeff Shore

Published with the support of a generous grant from
Hanazono University, Kyoto, Japan

ISBN
10 digit: 1-4379-7946-7
13 digit: 978-1-4379-7946-6

Diane Publishing Company

Contents

Contents

Dedicated to
Keidô Fukushima (1933–2011)
and
my twin sister Jean (1953–2011)

Foreword

This volume is based on a collection of Dharma talks given by Jeff Shore at Zen retreats in the U.S. and in Europe. Dharma talks are public discourses on Buddhism by a Buddhist teacher. I was privileged to take part in several of the retreats (at Pendle Hill Friends and St. Raphaela Retreat House, near Philadelphia) in which these talks were given. Jeff Shore is a native of the Philadelphia area, but has spent the past 30 years in Japan studying and teaching Zen Buddhism. Although he has completed Zen practice in the Rinzai training monastery of Tôfukuji in Kyoto, he is not a monk. Rather he follows the ancient tradition of Zen layman.

Jeff doesn't wear Buddhist robes or employ much in the way of Zen paraphernalia. He regards these as inappropriate for the West. At retreats, we do chant the verses of the *Four Great Vows* twice a day in Jeff's lucid translation.

> *Numberless beings – set free*
> *Endless delusion – let go*
> *Countless Dharma – see through*
> *Peerless Way – manifest!*

Jeff's retreats are demanding. Conducted in silence and lasting for around five days, zazen meditation of forty-minute periods each begin at around 5:30AM and continue till around 2:30AM the next morning. Each morning Jeff would give a lecture.

By the second day of a retreat, sleep would tug at me incessantly. But I remember always being alert for Jeff's talks. The lectures were by turns intellectually intriguing, and spiritually uplifting. Often they were, as well, great stories. When I read the talks, I can hear Jeff speaking in his clear, calm, manner, and can picture him seated with legs crossed on his cushion, so unlike the stern Zen masters of imagination.

Following the talks there would be a period in which to ask questions or make comments. Many of the talks centered on original translations of Zen poems. Jeff would often ask our opinion about word choice in the poems he was translating. In this way we had a sense that we were, in some small way, helping to create the translations.

To make his points, Jeff uses ideas ranging from the esoteric to the folksy. Paul Tillich and Meister Eckhart are quoted along with Broadway lyrics and Br'er Rabbit. To show us that Zen poetry isn't something only written by Chinese monks in the 10th century, he would quote Walt Whitman, who composed his verse a few miles from where we were sitting. In his interpretation of the Buddha's Fire Sermon, Jeff uses the contemporary story of a real forest firefighter, Wagner Dodge, who used a distinctly Zen approach to escape when surrounded by flames.

Before I heard him speak on the *Oxherding Pictures*, they were my least favorite piece of Buddhist literature. Naively, I saw the pictures as stages of spiritual progress with myself stuck in the first picture. Jeff tells us – Don't worry about keeping track of the stages. Don't worry about where you are in the pictures either. The first will do if you're really there.

Jeff frequently draws on Zen stories to explain the poem he has translated. For example, the story behind Baizhang's "A day without work is a day without eating" is wonderfully linked to verse seven of *Enjoying the Way*.

In his translation of *Enjoying the Way*, Jeff quotes Lazy Zan as saying

If a meal is offered, just gobble it up.

Jeff's retreat lectures are much too rich a meal to be gobbled. Read them slowly as we heard them read to us, over many days. Ponder them. Stop in your reading, as Jeff would do, to take a sip of tea. In so doing, you will be rewarded with an understanding of the insights of this wise and compassionate teacher.

Michael Halperin
Director, Lippincott Library
Wharton School, University of Pennsylvania

Preface
Guus van Osch

In this book Jeff Shore presents translations and commentaries on three classic Chinese Zen texts. One of them is quite well known (The Oxherding Pictures), the other two are not (Exhortations for Those Who Don't Arouse the Doubt and Enjoying the Way). Much of the material has never been translated before. The main goal of this book, however, is not academic or literary: it is to inspire, to encourage, to guide. Here is a Zen teacher using a venerated tradition (as commenting on classic Zen texts is) to provide us with authentic Zen texts and in-depth insight on what these classic texts really say and how they can be applied in the present day. These texts have been used – now and in the past – to actually guide Zen practitioners along the way. It is no surprise then that the basis of this book consists of Jeff's lectures during Zen retreats all over the world. The Appendix adds two more lectures, both vintage examples of Jeff's direct and down-to-earth approach. Together with the three classic texts, here is a solid presentation of living, contemporary Zen. The initial audiences consisted of Zen practitioners, young and old, first timers and old hands, sitting on meditation cushions on the floors of all kinds of zendos (meditation halls). Some were authentic Zen Buddhist zendos, some were located in Christian monasteries, others were mere attics. These retreats lasted for somewhere between three and seven days of intense sitting. Every day a lecture was given and every day there was at least one opportunity for every participant to meet Jeff for a private interview (called "one-on-one"). These one-on-ones provide an opportunity to clarify things, resolve doubts, or make sure you are on the right track. A lot of this living context is obviously "lost in translation" in the book. So in this introduction I will give the reader a taste of what actual Zen practice can be. While the texts presented all aim to illuminate the path of Zen practice and point out the proper direction, here I will try to shed some light on what it is to actually walk the path and be on the receiving end of all this guidance and pointing.

I met Jeff Shore in an attic serving as a Zen meditation hall in Utrecht, Netherlands. He was there to give a lecture but I only remember this occasion because he brought gifts from Japan. After the lecture he sat on the floor, opened his little cotton backpack and took out a couple of Japanese calligraphy prints called *shikishi*. "Take one you like," he said to us. When it was my turn I asked him to pick one for me. He chose one that had a calligraphy saying: "Ever clear and present."

This marked the beginning of a long and ever deepening spiritual friendship of well over a decade now. Many more questions have been asked and gifts given since that evening in Utrecht.

At the time I had just started doing Zen meditation and was having great difficulty just sitting still in half lotus for 25 minutes. The pain it caused has long been my companion in practice. I remember he once said to me that those who experience a lot of pain during zazen usually turn out to become stronger sitters than those who just flex their legs in full lotus without blinking an eye. At the time I thought this was a great comfort; now I think he just told the truth. I did not have a clear idea about why I wanted to do Zen meditation. I had trouble coming to terms with myself, the world, and my place in it. Zen just seemed a way to get away from all of that without me actually having to open up to anyone about my incapability and insecurity. I could just sit there, do this Zen thing and somewhere along the line things would get solved. It felt good to be part of a group with the same mission: sit hard and get enlightened. I felt like a member of some Special Forces unit, doing rigorous training at the most ungodly hours.

These were all pleasant thoughts while drinking tea – but the pain in my legs during zazen would not be softened by them. This reality stared me in the face every time I sat. After about two years it dawned on me: this is it. Guus is not going to be changed by this. He is still the same Guus sitting there, no miracle will happen. Yes, my legs had become slightly more flexible, but when I did my first full day of sitting zazen I was still – after two years – in a lot of pain. I was also still prone to bouts of depression, fear and insecurity. I could not escape from myself, even on a cushion, even chanting the *Heart Sutra*, even doing *kinhin* (walking meditation). No divine intervention, no good fairies. By now I knew that my pain could not be fooled by any trick or mantra; it could not be negotiated with. It demanded its full due and I had nowhere to go but to sit there and pay it. So the choice was simple: get up and leave this painful practice or stay put without any guarantees. A number of times I left, but every time I had not even closed the door behind me when I realized that my place was IN there. There simply was no other option: at least the pain in the zendo was supposed to be part of a 2,500 year old tradition that did promise liberation somewhere along the line. But I realized that it was Guus just the way he was who was going to go that whole long uncertain road...

What kept me going? I'm still not sure. All I know is that there was some deep yearning inside me to be free, to be whole, to be at peace. It was very hard to make it any more explicit. People asking me why I did Zen training always made me feel ill at ease. I sometimes felt a little guilty because I seemed not to have any Great or Deep Religious Question but just wanted the shit to end in my life. That couldn't be a good enough reason, could it? Was I willing to cut off my arm in order to get it? Maybe not quite yet, so where did that leave me? It took me some time to frankly admit to myself (and to Jeff during one-on-one) that, although the first vow to save all beings moved me to tears when chanting it, I was in it for my own happiness.

I had experienced enough moments of clarity, lightness during and after retreats but also knew that they all evaporate after some time. Was my quest(ion) religious or would a qualified therapist have been able to help me? Over the years I have met a lot of other people who first had to get rid of or heal some inner mental or emotional imbalance and only then could go on with Zen practice. Maybe this layer needs to be peeled away before one can fruitfully continue. And Zen practice might not be the best way to do this. The classic (monastic) Zen tradition does not seem to address the possible mental, psychological or relational problems modern man can experience. What to make of this? One of my former teachers used to say that Zen can be therapeutic but is not therapy in itself.

I've also met people who somehow seemed to be able to take a shortcut around their own issues and forge ahead regardless with their Zen training: some of them eventually come to a grinding halt, blaming Zen, its traditions or its teachers for the state their lives are in. However sad to witness, I believe that this can be a valuable and maybe even necessary part of getting to the core of Zen/yourself. We all start from where we are and continue from where we left off.

For me, Zen practice made me realize that I did need therapeutic help after all. Was I disappointed in Zen? No, frankly I was grateful for the insight. After the therapy ended I stopped sitting zazen for almost a year. It had become too much part of the old scenario of demands and standards I had to meet. I figured that if Zen was really my path, the actual practice would find its way back into my life without me dragging it in. And it did. Once again, the drive that put me back on my cushion still was virtually impossible to describe. I just knew that it was good for me. My wife used to say that Zen made me a lighter and at the same time a more grounded person.

So the first years of my Zen practice turned out to be a far more physical, bodily practice than I had thought. Of course my mind was not that disciplined either, but I was more bothered by the pain than by my unruly head. But sitting long hours with painful legs does have an impact on your mental constitution; the outer discipline of sitting zazen every day quite naturally leads to a kind of inner discipline developing. But it is a slow process. Every Zen book and every teacher will tell you to BE the pain, but just what that entails took me some years to see. The fear of pain is so deeply ingrained that the effort to consciously expose yourself to it is utterly counterintuitive. We keep turning away, desperately looking for a way out other than through the flames themselves. At that point it is easy to think that not being able to escape from it is due to some defect in your practice. This is where a teacher is invaluable. Someone who very simply shows that when you are fighting the pain you are creating a separation, trying to get away from your actual present reality and so are going in the opposite direction of where the practice needs to go: right here, just be one. So you go back to your cushion and before long you note that you are still doing it: pain comes, tension arises in your mind and body, and we're back at square one. Lost with the map in your hands.

What about the time-honored instruction of counting your breath? Well, that didn't go any better as everyone knows who has ever begun to do it. So, I kept failing on all accounts. But an interesting thing occurred: when you fail once, you hit yourself over the head. When you fail 10 times, you hit yourself over the head even harder. But what do you do when you fail 10,000 times? Eventually it becomes meaningless: you just start over. You realize that hitting yourself over the head does not improve anything but is just a waste of time. You become free from something and you realize that this does not only apply to zazen practice. You actually have learned – in my case without having the slightest clue while learning it – to let go of results, demands. For me that was an amazing realization. Once again this is where a teacher is crucial: showing a near infinite patience with your fruitless efforts, giving untiring advice on how to simply proceed, never giving up on you. My first teacher taught me a lot in this regard. During a lecture in the first *sesshin* (Zen retreat) that I did with him he quoted Paul Tillich: "Accept that you are accepted." That stuck with me and I went into *dokusan* (formal but personal interview) with him curious whether this small Asian guy would be able to not only say it but actually live it. He did. I suppose at the time he was capable of accepting me to a larger extent than I was capable of accepting myself. Was this a religious experience? I don't think so. But it was deeply liberating. My time with him allowed me to shed some old skin and continue along the path a changed man, even up to the point that, five years later, I was capable of accepting his rejecting me and leaving his sangha (community of Zen practitioners surrounding a teacher).

All this time Jeff had been a constant factor in my Zen practice. Every year we met at one or more of his retreats. And every time he kept pestering me in our one-on-ones: from "Where are you in your practice?" and "What drives you in your practice?" to "What is lacking?" So far, however, I still kept my distance. Not only because I had a different master, but somehow he was too severe for me. Not a personal severity, but he seemed to expect a commitment to practice that I was not up to. His was a direct and uncompromising way of getting to the bottom of yourself, as he likes to call it. As may have become clear from what I've written, that had been just a little too hardcore for me.

But there I was: fresh out of a sangha that I had been part of for almost five years, knowing full well that I was imperfect and having experienced first hand that a sangha is also imperfect – and also slowly realizing that a master is imperfect too (one of the best kept secrets in Zen, it seems). Yet all this imperfection did not prevent my practice from maturing. The pain was no longer an issue: finally having learned to surrender to it after deeply inquiring into what actually constitutes pain itself and what actually constitutes my response to it and getting lost at exactly that spot. Maybe this was what Jeff meant by being one with everything that was present? I had perfected the art of failure to the point that now even Jeff's approach to Zen practice no longer intimidated me. And there still was this nagging question: "**What is lacking?**"

Up to this point zazen had been for the most part a matter of working hard, pushing on and on, requiring willpower, perseverance and stamina. But once in a while, during one-on-one, I came away with the sense that this was maybe not the way to go. I remember Jeff one time saying to me: "You are still trying to **do** something." And I was; I was still trying to get away from this present moment, from this present Guus in order to get...where? Well, Nirvana, of course, kenshô, enlightenment, whatever you call it. But away from this unsatisfying, recurrent stop-and-go of happiness and suffering. *Terra firma* at last! *Bodhi swaha*! How many times I had read or come across the beautiful story of the butterfly caught in the temple bell, desperately trying to get out but failing at every attempt. Until, finally, completely exhausted it just couldn't fly anymore and dropped: out of the bell into the light. Yearning for a similar experience I would gather all my determination and strength and get going again. Completely oblivious of the fact that it was exactly this determination and striving that kept me enchained. "The ego can corrupt anything it comes into contact with," Jeff would quote Richard De-Martino, his teacher at university who introduced him to Zen. And everyone in the zendo solemnly nodded. Then he added, "Even zazen." All nodding stopped. Did I get it? Yes, I did, as you might also get it when you read this. Did getting it change anything? Nope. How can you give up wanting something that you deeply, desperately want, even when they tell you that by giving it up it will be yours? Jeff lectured on the *Oxherding Pictures* and for a while they will become your road map, despite Jeff warning us against it. Glad to finally have some signposts along this hazy path. Gauging where you are and trying to get to the next "level." But it is *déjà vu*. Wherever you are, that is where you are. Guus will be Guus. No bull. Never mind levels, never mind "progress." There is only the practice of the present.

"When nothing you do will do, then what do you do?" Japanese Zen layman Shin'ichi Hisamatsu asked, exactly pointing out the predicament Zen practitioners are in. "Stop the seeking mind that seeks to stop itself," Jeff chimes in. Enough already, OK? Every attempt at breaking through the wall only fortifies it, OK? You return from the small one-on-one room to the zendo, once again forget to bow at the entrance, then go in and sit down on your cushion. Yeah, you got it alright. Another dead end, that's what you got. Increasingly bewildered as to the direction you are now meant to go in, even of the nature of the effort you are now expected to make. This is the nature of Zen teaching, I think. Nothing really is taught, the student is just steered away from the wrong direction and effort. Every time you enter the one-on-one room with some precious, shining new insight or answer, you leave with empty hands. Once during the go around at the end of a retreat in Hungary, one of the participants called it being given a "brain-freeze" by Jeff during one-on-one. Eminently eloquent. At other times – after long, long hours, sometimes even sitting through the nights in dimly lit zendos – it is just a softly spoken "Don't give up" that brings tears to your eyes while walking back to your ever-patient cushion. And you don't give up, even though you are not sure what keeps you going. Is there something else that carries you while your own conscious willpower is slowly melting away, your own determined effort is being extinguished bit by bit? Questions that only arise afterwards because at the time you are just there: sitting, utterly not knowing. Great doubt, great faith and great determination? No idea, you just sit there – but it does sound rather accurate. Slowly, you learn to abide in this region where it is OK to just sit here, to just notice that every once in a while something inside you stirs and wants to be somewhere else, something else, someone else. You learn that all that is just something that comes and goes, comes and goes. Sometimes the color changes, sometimes the intensity, sometimes the frequency but it all is just coming and going. No need to hold on to any of it – you have done that all of your life and what did it bring you? It is like the fairy tale by Hans Christian Andersen about the little match girl. Short moments of warmth and light, but then it all just dies out again, cold and darkness returning. You learn that thinking the deepest thoughts or feeling the profoundest feelings is just more of the same: another match lit for as long as it lasts. Is it a coincidence that just around that time Jeff is lecturing on the *Exhortations* by Boshan? Boshan with his resounding and recurring reproof: "This too is just your wavering mind! It is not Zen!" Initially you might resist a little, but in the end you plead guilty on all charges.

In the meantime you may run into some old pain, some old scars and for a time you think that Buddhism is about healing those, about finally finding comfort within yourself. But thank Buddha for teachers. Sitting in their small one-on-one room or e-mailing you from the other side of the globe:

Dear Guus,
Being able to sit through your fear is valuable indeed. I trust you will continue to sit through, to the end. No need to try and rouse a certain state, such as fear. If it comes, fine. BE IT. If it doesn't, fine. Be fully present with whatever arises. But "keep your eye on the ball," the source of it all, not on the arising of thoughts and emotions, no matter how strong they may appear. As you have seen, they can uncover valuable things; they can also mask what is invaluable. Always here for you.

Gasshou [Palms together in gratefulness],
Jeff

The *Heart Sutra* starts to actually make some sense (remember how many times you chanted it, wholeheartedly yet completely ignorantly?) No eye, no ear, no nose.

So you just continue sitting, like a big fool, not knowing where it will lead you. You have all kinds of nice experiences and time and time again you are told to just let go of them, to move on. This can be rather difficult at times: of course you are aware that your zazen practice has matured, that it has deepened. So now you are even more intent on making this kenshô-thing happen to you. By now even you, reader without any Zen experience, will realize that this is exactly what gets in the way. In Zen terminology: the Gateless Barrier. Yes, possibly you get a glimpse or two; but then look what happens. You immediately turn it into the Holy Grail, "My little precious!" "THIS IS IT! NOW DON'T GO AND LOSE IT!" is all you can think about. And of course, like a sand castle on the beach, it slips away and you are left: mourning, cocky, confused. "It's nothing," your teacher says and you hate him for it. Don't you deserve it, didn't you earn it for all your long hours and long years of zazen? Are you not entitled to it, finally? "Smash the diamond," he says, and you know exactly what he means. Once again, blurry-eyed, you return to your ever faithful cushion.

All this too was some kind of phase I apparently needed to go through. The only way forward (notice how difficult it is to use words here without inadvertently implying that there is actually somewhere to go?) is to just continue sitting amidst this paradox. After having run around and tried all the possible exits, you not only understand that this is to no avail, it somehow seeps into your whole system. It is not just your mind that "gets it" – it is somehow realized by your body, by you as a whole. Zen practice is not about understanding, about "getting it." It is about actually coming to the end of seeking itself. It is not about letting go or accepting either because that still contains an element of me doing something about something outside (or inside) myself. It is not solving the paradox but becoming the paradox to the extent that paradox and sitter are inseparable. No, even that is incorrect: It is ultimately realizing that you ARE this paradox, you don't even have to become it. Then you are truly sitting in the dark. Utterly. You have by now tried all the emergency exits and they do not exist: what looked like exits are just re-entrances (granted, with a nice detour sometimes) into the same cycle of endlessly coming and going. Even these earlier wonderful glimpses have become faded memories. Once precious but now – again – getting in the way of the present moment, of this. Yet there you are; whatever you say to yourself, will not do. Whatever you do, will not do, whatever you think, feel, sense, remember, want, reject, are aware of – none of it will do. Yet there you are.

And there is your teacher, whispering: "Don't give up." Beyond tears now, you return to your cushion and sit: one solid block of doubt, to use another Zen term. If you stop turning over the hourglass, it will empty out by itself. Then what can you say? Can words even reach there?

Reading Lazy Zan's *Enjoying the Way* you marvel at his carefree song. Fearlessly using words where you barely dare to stammer. It is like the information labels on the back of wine bottles. How do they relate to the actual taste of the wine, the actual experience of it? Whatever I have written is just words, just labels, not a drop of wine in there. And yet that is precisely what it is all about: to just simply taste this (utterly inconceivable, "un-gettable") wine and be done with labels.

What is true tasting? Who is able to teach that? Do we need to be taught such a thing? As the Zen saying goes: the family jewels do not enter through the gate. The most eloquent description is not even close to taking an actual sip. Which do you prefer: the label or the sip? Which do you genuinely yearn for? Then go for that. Give yourself to it as fully and totally and completely as it gives itself to you. Then it is like a gift: "Ever clear and present."

This book is a valuable guide along the way. Jeff Shore not only clarifies the value of true and sustained Zen practice, he embodies it; his lectures are both originating from it and pointing towards it. He urges us to sincerely dedicate ourselves to Zen practice. His words encourage, point, warn, celebrate, comfort and inspire. I sincerely hope that reading this book will result in putting it aside and returning you to your ever-patient cushion. Not a second of practice will ever go to waste.

Gasshou

Conventions and Abbreviations

Chinese names for major figures are given in simplified Pinyin followed by the Japanese reading and Chinese characters. Terms commonly known by their Wade-Giles reading are given in Pinyin, followed by simplified Wade-Giles, such as *Dao De Jing (Tao Te Ching) and Zhuangzi (Chuang Tzu).* Japanese persons living after the Meiji Reforms of 1868 are written with family name last, as in Keidô Fukushima and Zenkei Shibayama.

BCR   *The Blue Cliff Record,* Thomas and J. C. Cleary translators (Boston: Shambhala, 1992).

BUS   "The 'Short-cut' Approach of *K'an-hua* Meditation" Robert E. Buswell, Jr. in *Sudden and Gradual: Approaches to Enlightenment in Chinese Thought,* Peter N. Gregory Editor (Honolulu: University of Hawaii Press, 1988).

BWS   *Being Without Self: Zen for the Modern World,* Jeff Shore (Rotterdam: Asoka, 2008).

CB   *The Courage to Be,* Paul Tillich (New Haven: Yale University Press, 1971).

d.   died

DHP   *Dhammapada.*

ED   *Enlightenment in Dispute: The Reinvention of Chan Buddhism in Seventeenth-Century China,* Jiang Wu (New York: Oxford University Press, 2008).

ET   *The Essential Teachings of Zen Master Hakuin,* Norman Waddell (Boston: Shambhala, 1994).

EV   *Entangling Vines: Zen Koans of the Shûmon Kattôshû,* Thomas Yûhô Kirchner translator (Kyoto: Tenryu-ji Institute for Philosophy and Religion, 2004).

HP   *Hakuin's Precious Mirror Cave,* Norman Waddell translator (Berkeley: Counterpoint, 2009).

IA   *The Zen Teaching of Instantaneous Awakening,* John Blofeld translator (Leicester: Buddhist Publishing Group, 1987).

LB   *The Life of Buddha,* Edward J. Thomas, (London: Routledge & Kegan Paul, 1975).

ME   *Meister Eckhart and the Beguine Mystics,* Bernard McGinn (New York: Continuum, 2001).

MK   *Meditating With Koans,* J. C. Cleary translator (Berkeley: Asian Humanities Press, 1992).

ML	*Mystical Languages of Unsaying*, Michael A. Sells (Chicago: University of Chicago Press, 1994).
MT	*The Mystical Thought of Meister Eckhart: The Man From Whom God Hid Nothing*, Bernard McGinn (New York: Crossroad Publishing Company, 2001).
OTS	*The Old Tea Seller*, Norman Waddell (Berkeley: Counterpoint, 2008).
PZ	*The Practice of Zen*, Chang Chen-chi (New York: Harper & Brothers, 1959).
RAH	*The Religious Art of Zen Master Hakuin*, Katsuhiro Yoshizawa (Berkeley: Counterpoint, 2009).
rev.	revised
RL	*The Record of Linji*, Ruth Fuller Sasaki translator (Honolulu: University of Hawaii Press, 2009).
SB	*Sun Face Buddha: The Teachings of Ma-tsu and the Hung-chou School of Ch'an*, Cheng Chien Bhikshu translator (Berkeley: Asian Humanities Press, 1992).
SF	*Swampland Flowers: The Letters and Lectures of Zen Master Ta Hui*, Christopher Cleary translator (New York: Grove Press, 1977).
SLP	*The Sayings of Layman P'ang: A Zen Classic of China*, James Green translator (Boston: Shambhala, 2009).
ST	*Systematic Theology* Volume 2, Paul Tillich (Chicago: University of Chicago Press, 1957).
T	大正新脩大蔵經 (CBETA Chinese Electronic Tripitaka, Normalized Version).
TO	*The Ten Oxherding Pictures*, Mumon Yamada (Honolulu: University of Hawaii Press, 2004).
UB	*The Unborn: The Life and Teaching of Zen Master Bankei*, Norman Waddell translator (San Francisco: North Point Press, 1984).
UW	*The Unspoken Word: Negative Theology in Meister Eckhart's German Sermons*, Bruce Milem (Washington D. C.: Catholic University of America Press, 2002).
WI	*Wild Ivy: The Spiritual Autobiography of Zen Master Hakuin*, Norman Waddell translator (Boston: Shambhala, 1999).
WJ	*Wandering Joy: Meister Eckhart's Mystical Philosophy*, Reiner Schürmann (Great Barrington: Lindisfarne Books, 2001).
WL	"The Wasteland" in *Selected Poems*, T. S. Eliot (London: Faber and Faber, 1961).

WT	*Wen-tzu: Understanding the Mysteries,* Thomas Cleary translator (Boston: Shambhala, 1992).
X	卍新纂續藏經 (CBETA Chinese Electronic Tripitaka, Normalized Version).
ZB	**Zen and the Taming of the Bull: Towards a Definition of Buddhist Thought**, Walpola Rahula (London: Gordon Fraser, 1978).
ZCM	*Zen Comments on the Mumonkan [Gateless Barrier],* Zenkei Shibayama (New York: Harper & Row, 1974).
ZD	*Zen Dust: The History of the Koan and Koan Study in Rinzai (Lin-chi) Zen,* Isshû Miura and Ruth Fuller Sasaki (New York: Harcourt, Brace & World, 1966).
ZM	*Zongmi on Chan,* Jeffrey Lyle Broughton (New York: Columbia University Press, 2009).
ZMH	*The Zen Master Hakuin: Selected Writings,* Philip B. Yampolsky translator (New York: Columbia University Press, 1971).
ZS	*Zen Sand: The Book of Capping Phrases for Kôan Practice,* Victor Sôgen Hori translator (Honolulu: University of Hawaii Press, 2003).
盤珪	『盤珪禅師全集』赤尾龍治 (東京: 大蔵出版, 1976).
馬録	『馬祖の語録』入矢義高編 (京都: 禅文化研究所, 1984).
虚堂	『國譯虚堂和尚語録』国訳禅宗叢書、第六 (東京：国訳禅宗叢書刊行会, 1974).
遠羅	『遠羅天釜』白隠慧鶴, 芳澤勝弘訳注 (京都: 禅文化研究所, 2001).
禅関	『禅関策進』禅の語録19, 藤吉慈海 (東京: 筑摩書房, 1970).

Introduction:
Encountering the First Vow

Jack Vartabedian

Popular Buddhist phrases like "no-self" or "no-soul" sound alarmingly imper-sonal. Even Mahayana Buddhism's compassionate Bodhisattva ideal – vowing to postpone Nirvana until all beings are free – is found lacking once we learn that this ideal rejects the reality of a being or personality or separated individuality. It is natural to harbor the suspicion that seekers drawn to a tradition like Buddhism are both desperate and dishonest. Desperately unable to stomach the appearance of beings or individuals endlessly failing to find what they are looking for, Buddhist seekers are reduced to *lying* their way out of the problem. True peace, they say, is realizing that the obvious – the "being" or "individual" who suffers – is an illusion: there are no beings to free. But whether or not there ultimately is a being, self, or soul that suffers, the historically present fact of "some unhappiness somewhere" cannot be lied away, and neither can the need to end that suffering.

Familiar with this suspicion towards Buddhism I had the fortune to meet Jeff Shore. Remaining critical of bookstore or popular Buddhism, I was sympathetic to a basic insight: If there is an historical end to suffering, that end is brought about through the *loss* encountered in silence and solitude. Unfortunately, most popular works on Buddhism (and Christianity) reveal teachers who fail to appreciate both that loss and the corresponding (and mysterious) *total* assumption of responsibil-ity for the existence of suffering. Jeff was the first teacher I encountered who was consistently silent about "individual" practice and responsibility. There was, and is, an obvious sense of responsibility for the suffering of *all* that his *immediate* practice assumes. I wanted to know what that was.

My eventual encounter with Jeff's compassion was brought about through a frustrating failure to encounter anything like it in Christianity or western philoso-phy. Though from a young age I found it easy to pray and experience or "receive" what I called the unconditional love of Christ, it became increasingly impossible to accept the absence of that love in myself towards others, an absence I also discov-ered in the Jesus of the Gospels who often referred to Hell and Final Judgment.

My real searching began after graduating from Davidson College in 1993 with a degree in Economics. Eventually landing a job as a market maker on the op-tions floor of the Philadelphia Stock Exchange, my life became a contradiction: Naturally turned off by the idea of offering a service (teaching, sales, medicine, law, etc.) while getting paid for it, I eventually made my living underground (literally underneath Market Street) standing in a "crowd," trading derivatives – an honest and therefore not very benevolent form of capitalism. No less sincere, however, was my interest in what I knew as the absolute benevolence of Christ, along with the Gospels, the Orthodox Church, and the monastic writings of Thomas Merton. As I gradually became convinced that a life committed to the cultivation of uncondi-tional love was the only life worth living, there was a corresponding need to find the right conditions – mental and material – for cultivating it, and it was obvious that I would never find them in my job, my church, the Gospels, nor Thomas Merton. So in the summer of 1999 I quit my honest job on the Exchange and for the next 9 years did nothing but throw myself into western philosophy.

Along the way I caved in to the possibility of professional teaching at an accredited academic institution. In 2001 I received a scholarship to the graduate philosophy program at the Catholic University of America in Washington, D.C., where I completed all Masters requirements and all course work for the Ph.D. While preparing for the Ph.D. reading list and foreign language exams, I began teaching as an adjunct at Mount Saint Mary's University in Emmitsburg, Maryland. This is where one phase of my life came to an end. In the beginning of my second year teaching it finally became clear that my desire to stay connected to credible institutions of any kind was a major hindrance to what I needed to do. I dropped out of the Ph.D. program at Catholic, and gave notice to the head of the department at the Mount. I wrote an email to Jeff Shore, who I had met only once, telling him that I was quitting my job in order to throw myself into the practice of zazen (which I started two years prior). I have been happily waiting tables ever since.

Making a long story short, all this work in philosophy made one thing clear: whatever it was that I knew in prayer and was fueling my searching – call it Christ or the Father – it assumed complete responsibility for relieving the suffering of the world, and I could not find this total sense of responsibility in anyone I encountered or read. Prayer at times revealed a joy and love that felt like it was the true source of everything, that no one could refuse, and that could satisfy anyone. This *irresistible* love and joy was for me what the name "Christ" referred to. But it also became clear that the mainstream educational institutions, including Protestant, Orthodox, and Catholic Churches – along with the Biblical Jesus – were too comfortable either talking to or (worse) *threatening* the "unsaved," instead of just shutting up and freeing them. So it was necessary to leave these institutions behind, at least for a while. It was even more necessary to find out where to go.

Though academic philosophy caters more to vanity and pride than to what really drives us, I don't see how I could have entered religious life with any kind of integrity without the work I did there. For someone who senses or feels that unconditional irresistible love is the source of all, there's a reconciliation *with appearances* that has to take place. How do you reconcile the fact that the apparent world of endless searching and unhappiness clearly *is* resisting its irresistible source? There are essentially two steps involved, both of which pertain to a genuinely religious assumption of responsibility: First, to realize that genuine happiness is not one option among others; it's the only option. Anyone, therefore, who is not genuinely happy is not choosing to be that way, but is simply unable to fully appreciate what needs to be done. So whatever the reason for the apparent resistance to irresistible happiness or love, there's no putting responsibility for it on individuals. This conclusion turns our ordinary sense of free will/responsibility and blame upside down.

Second, one realizes that this immediate irresistible joyful source of it all cannot itself be *causal* (one thing or state bringing about another thing or state). Why not? Because where there are causes and effects *like comes from like*, and thus any cause whose effect is a world susceptible to the heartless dissatisfaction of the apparent world must itself *be* susceptible to heartlessness and dissatisfaction. But if we see this, whether we like it or not, we are forced to discover this Cause of the world of suffering immediately in ourselves: Individuating – willing to be happy while others in the world are not, loving others conditionally, endlessly issuing commands for others to obey – all are turned away from Unconditional Love. All must return to it. The reconciliation of the apparent world with its source must be made from here, where our *total* responsibility for the fact of suffering is discovered in an ultimate individuating hardness of heart, and where, quite in spite of this, a mysterious and complete responsibility for the alleviation of suffering has been assumed. Either all return, or there is no return. That's all we know. Good philosophizing can help us "see" this responsibility, but diving into it requires more.

With my Theistic/Christian background and problem, I had the good fortune to discover a retreat talk entitled "Principles of Zen Practice" given by Jeff Shore. Here Jeff encourages precisely the sense of responsibility I believed I was looking for, though he expressed it as the first vow of the Bodhisattva:

> Why do we sit zazen? For you? For me? The typical Mahayana answer is: for all beings. Isn't that strange? Can't we sit here and get it for ourselves first and then maybe we can think about somebody else? Doesn't that make sense – you've got to do it yourself first, right? But Buddhism, especially Mahayana Buddhism, states that we *begin* our practice from the standpoint of all beings. Why? Because that's the only place we *can* practice. The source of present awareness is inseparable from all beings. It must include all beings.

> (*BWS*, 95)

All searching up to this point had made me aware that the lack of complete happiness anywhere in the world was somehow right here in "my" present awareness, I didn't feel separate from the unhappiness of others. Jeff here was pointing at something inseparable – the source of present awareness – that brings an end to that universal lack. This was neither the Buddhism nor the Christianity I was familiar with, both of which (at least on the surface) teach that each of us is individually responsible for our own salvation, and the most we can do with regard to others is encourage others to practice, and hope for the best. But as this passage makes clear, if there is such a thing as salvation and a way to it, "it must include all beings" – right here and now. For me this meant that a genuine return to the source returns *all* to the source. That is, "your" practice (when engaged in properly) isn't yours at all, but something total and without individuation. It is the practice of everything. It frees or saves everything.

If we turn to the first oxherding picture, we can appreciate that what is being referred to is not the realization of an individual seeker, of his own individual sense of alienation. It's the alienation of all. As the caption reads, *all* is lost:

> *Turning away, the split occurs*
> **Covered in dust, finally all is lost.**
> *Hills of home ever more distant,*
> *Diverging paths proliferate:*
> *Flames of gain-loss,*
> *Blades of right-wrong.*
>
> *Wading through thick weeds, searching, searching.*
> *Rivers swell, mountains tower, paths unending.*
> *Exhausted, in despair, without a clue....*

But once we realize that all is lost, that all is endless searching, we are in the position to begin practice. We begin where the above quoted caption really begins:

> *Never gone astray —*
> *What need to search?*

Discovering that there's nowhere all *can* go is the way to realize that there's nowhere all *need* to go. As we realize that life for all is endless cycles of searching and suffering, all searching is brought to an end, and nothing anywhere is needed.

Do we lie to ourselves in the end — realizing that what was needed never went astray? Or do we lie to ourselves in the beginning, when we think it has gone astray? The second series of talks in this book, on Boshan's *Exhortations*, was the least liked by many retreat participants precisely because it encourages us not to lie to ourselves. No matter how desperate one's situation before committing to zazen, those who commit their whole life to a *method of resolution* are always more desperate to tell themselves that the problem is over: "I've awakened. Now I can just live my life and help others." But as Hakuin (and Boshan in his own way) puts it, "Oh that it were so easy!" If you have a sense of humor, you will need it. Nothing is more ridiculous (and frequent) than the lies we tell ourselves, fearing the genuine love and joy we are at bottom. If we're not desperate to claim an end to our problem too soon, we're desperate to create a problem right here where there isn't one. Zazen is the most simple, honest practice a person can engage in. But our complexity and dishonesty doesn't die easy.

This is where a genuine teacher from a living tradition is most helpful, and where the deeply personal nature of Buddhist practice and realization comes to life. Jeff Shore was not raised in a Buddhist culture and had no interest in becoming a Zen Master. He's just a guy from Philly with a serious personal need to find a happiness that went beyond the impermanence and unpredictability of bodily health, mental states, ideas, personal relationships, career, and hobbies, and who saw some hope in what little he could find on Zen Buddhism. After almost ten years of study and practice, he left home for good at the age of 27 and moved to Japan. Anyone that desperate won't be appeased by some publicly sanctioned figurehead who has no genuine acquaintance with either the problem or the solution. Though not "individual," the problem is personal – it concerns an immediately apparent demand for the happiness of all, and you can tell when you've met someone who is *more* acquainted with it than you are, and who has been *more* uncompromising about it than you have been. You meet someone like this and you know that in spite of being consumed with a problem, you've only been screwing around. This meeting is the happiest day of your life. You're scared too. This happy encounter pushes you into asking yourself, "How much am I *really* willing to lose?" You know it's not a game anymore, even though you never really thought it was.

Once the reader has made it to the third series of lectures on "Enjoying the Way," especially after the second series' emphasis on great doubt, I think he or she can't help but feel inspired. Whatever "no-self" is referring to, there is some kind of ultimate joy right here where we are, no matter what the apparent conditions. Such inspiration is precious and continues to arise with sustained practice, though it may also be accompanied by a subtle, false sense of complacency. The two talks presented in the Appendix: "The Constant Practice of Right Effort" and "Clarifying the Mind of Nirvana" will prove illuminating indeed to the reader unclear about the importance and difficulty of avoiding both self-complacency masked as Nirvana and self-aggrandizement parading as right effort. If you're unsure of what "self" and "no-self" refers to, you are probably more honest than 99 percent of those who feel very comfortable throwing those expressions around. That honesty combined with a little faith is all that is needed. I think you will find that there's nothing impersonal about it.

As I see it now, only a genuine encounter with the irresistible Father or Vow of the Bodhisattva can make the *impersonal* hardhearted sinfulness of separate being – or self – clear to us. Though it's very popular these days for Christians (including myself) to ignore the God of the Old Testament, it is perhaps more honest to face Him and see how much we resemble Him: We are happy with the good things even though others lack them. We love conditionally. We have "our people" who matter most to us, who are everything we want them to be, and whom we threaten or reject the moment they are no longer happy with that. We have no idea how to act without being a cause that brings about effects. And anything we have ever created or seen has been susceptible to damage. An honest look at Him reveals that we are not *estranged* from this Old Testament Creator/Cause. We *are* Him.

But once the irresistible Source or Father of all breaks through, what remains of self – the Creator/Separator – can no longer point at anything separate for what still appears to be wrong with the world. Instead, we can look upon the spectacle of misery that nature and the world is, knowing "I Am" *is* this misery. Encountering personal Unconditional Love, the impersonal Creator/Separator finds Himself to be a heartless, dissatisfied error, and the totality of His Being is given up through a kind of primordial repentance. Right here All is at the Source – in the midst of

Redemptive activity. For someone with strong roots in the Christian tradition, I would describe the zazen one learns with Jeff as the effortless practice of redeeming the entire world in Great Silence, or, in Zen terms, *before a word is spoken*. This is where the vow to free all beings comes from. Nothing could be more personal. May the reader be inspired to see this for himself.

No Bull:
Zen Oxherding Pictures

In the Zen tradition, oxherding pictures illustrate the process of religious discipline and awakening. The pictures presented here, along with narrative verse, depict this process in ten discrete steps or stages, outlining major transitions and warning of dangers along the way.

Comparisons have been made with Tibetan Buddhist depictions of the nine stages of elephant training. In popular legend, when Gotama (Sanskrit: Gautama) Buddha was conceived, his mother dreamed that a sacred white elephant entered her womb. Also, Gotama Buddha's taming of a wild elephant, which had been sent by Devadatta to kill Gotama, is a common subject of Buddhist art. According to early Pali Buddhist commentaries:

> *Just as a man would tie to a post*
> *A calf that should be tamed,*
> *Even so here should one tie one's own mind*
> *Tight to the object of mindfulness.*
> [Cited in ZB 16]

The metaphor is an ancient one. In China and in much of Southeast Asia, the farmer's ox was a fitting choice of subject since it was necessary for his livelihood. When the ox is gone, what is most essential has been lost. Like a mother unable to find her baby, or an American businessman who can't find where he parked his car (with laptop and wallet inside), one cannot have a moment's rest until it is found.

The ten paintings reproduced here are attributed to the Japanese Zen monk Shûbun [周文], a fifteenth-century abbot of the Shôkokuji Rinzai monastery complex in Kyoto and one of the greatest painters of his age. Each picture is accompanied by two short verses attributed to Guoan Shiyuan [Kakuan Shion 廓庵師遠], a Chinese Zen monk of the twelfth-century Song Dynasty. These verses have become a standard text in the Zen tradition and are included in the classic *Four Texts of the Zen School* [禪宗四部録] and in the two-volume *Poison-Painted Drum* [塗毒鼓], the handbook for Rinzai monastic practice. The calligraphy of the verses presented here was done by the Japanese monk Zekkai Chûshin [絶海中津 1336-1405] of the Muromachi Period and is designated an Important Cultural Property.

The verses for each picture are written in classical Chinese. First, there is a sort of prose poem, which sets the basic tone for each picture. (These have also been attributed to Guoan's disciple Ziyuan [Jion], who wrote an introduction to the ten *Oxherding Pictures*.) These prose poems are written in eight lines of verse, with the following number of Chinese characters for each line: 4, 4, 6, 6, 4, 4, 4, 4. Following each prose poem is a four-line poem of seven characters each, evoking the basic sentiment and fleshing it out, often with concrete sights and sounds.

The line scheme is maintained in the translation here – each line of Chinese is rendered as one line in English. However, I have made no attempt to follow the rhyme scheme, let alone the parallelism, antithesis, tones, and so on used in such verse. This is a retreat, not a conference or seminar; my focus throughout is

1

to expose the marrow, which is often only suggested, so that you can **see through your self**.

Don't worry about keeping track of the stages; just take in each one as a whole. Don't worry about where you are in the pictures either – the first one will do if you're really there.

Finally, the verse is terse and sometimes leaves unstated such basic components of syntax as subject, object, and verb. I trust that the reason for my clumsy attempt to do this in English will become clear as the lectures progress in this, the year of the ox (2009).

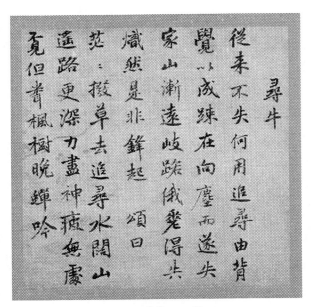

1. Seeking Ox

Never gone astray –
What need to search?
Turning away, the split occurs:
Covered in dust, finally all is lost.
Hills of home ever more distant,
Diverging paths proliferate:
Flames of gain-loss,
Blades of right-wrong.

Wading through thick weeds, searching, searching.
Rivers swell, mountains tower, paths unending.
Exhausted, in despair, without a clue.
Only the drone of cicadas in autumn leaves.

The first two lines throw us right into the maelstrom: If it's never gone astray, why search? If it ain't broke, why fix it? Even today, commentaries endlessly repeat that the young oxherder is you, the person seeking the Way, and that the ox is your true self, Buddha nature, the ultimate. But this is of little help. Who, after all, is the one seeking – and what, in the end, has been lost? If you knew that, you really wouldn't need to seek.

Yet here you are, seeking. Until you've really struggled with this and come to the end, to glibly say "It's never gone astray, so I don't need to search" is at best a half-truth, at worst a self-serving lie, isn't it?

In the picture, it's all eloquently expressed in the bearing of the farm boy-acolyte monk: Feet are carrying him off in one direction while head turns the other way. Split, within and without, doesn't know whether he's coming or going. Des-

4

perately searching – but no idea where to look.

The first two lines have already revealed that originally – when and where is that? – there is no you here, no ox there. Then the third line states why, if you're honest with yourself, you must seek, you cannot help but search: because reality has turned away from (literally "due to turning back on") its awakened-source. **Coming to my self**, I divert, pervert, what originally is. Thus the world of discrimination arises: self-other, enlightenment-illusion, life-death, right-wrong, and so on.

No reason is given for this original turning away. It is simply stated as a fact – a fact that each of us confirms in our experience of self.

Do you see a connection with the Fall in the Book of Genesis, with Adam and Eve (that is, all of us) turning away from God's command, thus opening their eyes and knowing they were naked? In his *Systematic Theology*, Paul Tillich explains it this way:

> The state of existence is the state of estrangement. Man is estranged from the ground of his being, from other beings, and from himself. ...Man as he exists is not what he essentially is and ought to be. He is estranged from his true being.
>
> [*ST* 44-45]

Tillich describes unbelief or "un-faith" this way:

> ...man in the totality of his being turns away from God. In his existential self-realization he turns toward himself and his world and loses his essential unity with the ground of his being and his world. ...Man, in actualizing himself, turns to himself and away from God in knowledge, will, and emotion.
>
> [*ST* 47]

The rest of the text for the first picture details this split into within and without: Covered in the defiling dust of sense-attachments (the five senses and mind), **the all is lost**. The further I seek, the more paths proliferate, with no sign of the desired object anywhere. At the same time, my home recedes further and further from view. Anxiety over gain and loss burns in my heart; dilemmas over what is right and wrong pierce my very soul.

The four-line poem continues the imagery: stuck in the mud and weeds of delusive attachment, rivers overflow their banks, vast peaks threaten from above. All my energy spent, stuck between a rock and a hard place, an oppressive, monotonous drone is all that the senses pick up.

Jackson Browne's classic rock anthem "Running on Empty" was recorded in 1977, a year after the suicide of his first wife:

> *Looking out at the road rushing under my wheels*
> *Looking back at the years gone by like so many summer fields*
> *In 'sixty-five I was seventeen and running up one-o-one*

5

I don't know where I'm running now, I'm just running on

Running on – running on empty
Running on – running blind
Running on – running into the sun
But I'm running behind

…. In 'sixty-nine I was twenty-one and I called the road my own
I don't know when that road turned onto the road I'm on

…. Looking out at the road rushing under my wheels
I don't know how to tell you just how crazy this life feels
I look around for the friends that I used to turn to to pull me through
Looking into their eyes I see them running too

…. You know I don't even know what I'm hoping to find
Running into the sun but I'm running behind

Sound familiar? This is where the journey begins. For an important discovery has already been made: I realize I have lost it. And in my restless seeking, I have become utterly lost. This is the point of the first picture, "Seeking Ox."

No longer feigning contentment with my discontent, I sincerely begin. I don't pretend that the bull is in the barn, don't divert my eye from the horns of the dilemma that I am. I no longer delude myself with wishy-washy, half-baked notions of delusion being enlightenment. I recognize that greedily seeking some enlightenment experience that's supposed to solve all my problems is, indeed, **a big problem**. Instead of "Seeking Ox," this first stage could be called "No More Bull."

In the 1946 film *Song of the South*, Br'er Rabbit, wandering happily on a country trail, gets in a tussle with a tar baby. (He has mistaken a couple of sticks covered in hot tar for a human.) Trying to get unstuck, Br'er Rabbit ends up getting "so stuck he can hardly move his eyeballs!"

Profound and pervasive dissatisfaction is common at this point; whatever we encounter, **that's not it**. As Paul Tillich succinctly put it: "Everything is tried and nothing satisfies." [*CB* 48] Every path breaks into ever more trails, without a clue or track to follow. Each path taken seems endless – yet ends up a dead end. The harder we try to find our way, the more lost we get. The first two noble truths of Buddhism manifest: blind craving inevitably results in *dis-ease*. Pursued in all sincerity, Great Doubt cannot but arise, for self **is** this split, this separation. The religious quest is not in vain; at this point in the journey, however, it sure as hell can seem like it.

The line "Flames of gain-loss" harks back to one of Gotama's first and foremost teachings, known as the Fire Sermon. (T. S. Eliot, in a note to "The Fire Sermon" section of his 1922 poem *The Waste Land*, goes so far as to state that this sermon "corresponds in importance to the Sermon on the Mount." [*WL* 72]) Addressing a group of fire-worshipping ascetics, Gotama turns up the heat by stating that all is burning, all is ablaze with blind desire, self-centered delusion, *dis-ease*. Later, we will return to this sermon and see what Gotama's got cooking.

During the extremely hot and dry August of 1949, a fire started in the mountains around Mann Gulch in central Montana. A group of firefighters led by Wagner Dodge is parachuted into the area. Rugged mountains rise on both sides of the valley. The fire is above them. In an emergency, they can safely retreat to the Missouri River at the bottom of the valley. The winds whip up debris, however, and a fire now starts **below** them, blocking the way to the river. Owing to freak weather conditions, this fire quickly grows into an enormous roaring wall of flame racing toward them much faster than they can run. Virtually impenetrable mountain slopes on both sides, fire raging above and below. Leader Dodge realizes they have not more than a minute or two before the inferno hits them.

What does he do? What do you do when things get too hot? We will return to Wagner Dodge later. Now I will let you stew in your own juices, to confirm for yourself the first oxherding picture. Then it will be time for us to take up the second picture.

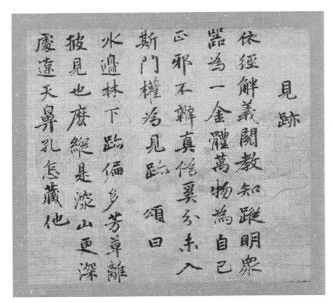

2. Seeing Traces

Through sutras, the meaning is understood,
Looking into the teachings, traces are found.
It's clear: various vessels are all one metal,
All things are one self.
But unable to tell right from wrong,
How to discern the true from the false?
Not yet having entered the gate,
At least the traces have been seen.

Tracks scattered all over the riverbank, under trees.
Thick in sweet grass — Ah! What's that?
However deep in the mountain depths,
Snout reaching heaven, nothing can conceal it.

Look at the picture: head is screwed on straight now, body and mind unified, hand firm on the rope of discipline.

What has happened? Tracks have been found! In the first picture, there was not a trace. Now the tracks are all around. The first two lines credit the sutras and teachings, and such is often the case. Many first find their feet through a sutra or a book on Buddhism or by encountering someone who has already made the trek.

Buddhist writings and Dharma encounters are indeed precious, as are encounters with other religions. But where, in fact, are the true teachings found? Keep heart and eye open.

Coming into contact with the Dharma (living truth) is not just a matter of reading books or listening to lectures — or even sitting in meditation. Dharma is not simply something you **do**. It must be what you **are**.

10

In giving your self completely to proper and sustained practice, a thread is found; fashioning it into a rope, diligently follow. The third and fourth lines reveal that one thread runs through all, that "all things are one self" – what is that?

Like the tracks themselves, the experience of this tends to remain a discrete event. So you're not yet able to discern the wheat from the chaff, the true from the false, as the fifth and sixth lines demonstrate. To sum up the second picture: the discrete tracks have clearly been seen, but the gate has not yet been entered.

The four-line poem tells that traces abound. The entangling weeds and mud have now transformed into sweet grass. Suddenly something stirs. Where is it? – Within? Without? Nowhere? Everywhere? We cannot lose sight of it again. Nothing can conceal what has been revealed. Whatever happens now, we remain hot on the trail:

> I have often walked down this street before;
> But the pavement always stayed beneath my feet before.
> All at once am I several stories high.
> Knowing I'm on the street where you live.
>> ["On the Street Where You Live" lyrics by
>> Alan Jay Learner, *My Fair Lady*, 1964]

In the Fire Sermon, Gotama described all as burning with desire, delusion, and *dis-ease*. In following the Way, the sermon continues, I become disenchanted and then dispassionate of **the all**. (Do you see? This is not merely self, seeking an experience that will solve its problems.) Then there can be full release. With full release, there is direct knowledge of release, and one discerns that this is the end of birth (and death), that the task has been done, that there is nothing further for this world. The Fire Sermon is a quintessential early Buddhist teaching of Nibbana [Sanskrit: Nirvana]: the flame of self extinguished.

Is that the only approach though? What about the contemplative consumed in the flame of God's love, or the Bodhisattva burning with compassion for all? Remember Wagner Dodge? With the flames fast approaching and nowhere to escape, what did he do?

First of all, he stopped running. That's right, stopped in his tracks. Have you? That is how to approach. By no longer running toward – or away from – **anything**, the tracks become clear. The way opens up underfoot. Strange as it sounds, if we don't stop, we can't truly proceed.

To stop is not merely to sit still. It is self, body-mind in its entirety, all the senses, coming to a full and complete stop. This is the beginning of true zazen.

Only when all running away – or toward – has ended, does it start to become clear. True religious practice is not an escape from our problems, psychological or otherwise. See for yourself: trying to **have it your way** – or get **a-way** – only gets **in** the way, creates more entanglements. In proper and sustained practice, let it all go, once and for all. With this second picture, "Seeing Traces," the right direction has been found.

But the gate has not yet been entered. Be careful here. Consciousness can be clarified, purified, emptied to an incredible degree. This can be most helpful as a preliminary practice. But that is far from the end of the matter. Learning to coast and enjoy the ride for a while is not coming to a full and complete stop. A clarified, purified consciousness emptied of its ordinary content is still discriminating consciousness. Discrimination is not discernment. It is a discursive, bifurcating symptom of *dis-ease*. And discernment is not merely discrimination. It is seeing into, seeing through, the true nature of things. Buddhism warns against both "false discrimination" and "false sameness." I leave it to you to discern the value of the so-called Zen, Buddhist, and other spiritual teachings flooding the market nowadays. The poem for case twelve of *Gateless Barrier* sums it up:

> *Those who search for the Way do not realize the Truth,*
> *They only know their old discriminating consciousness.*
> *This is the cause of the endless cycle of birth and death,*
> *Yet ignorant people take it for the Original Man.*
>
> [*ZCM* 91]

Many so-called teachers reduce the problem to dualistic thought or discriminating intellect and then offer ways to get rid of it – a sure sign that discrimination remains. Discriminating intellect is not the problem; it is merely the tip of the iceberg. As Paul Tillich already made clear, estrangement concerns "knowledge, will, and emotion." Whether thinking, willing, or feeling, self-as-consciousness is split. Do such teachers even recognize the real problem underfoot?

Don't mistake the footprint for the beast. Once you have stopped, **that which is sought in all sincerity shows the way.** The tracks unmistakably show the direction you must go.

In your practice, patiently gather all your energy into one. As you do, the activation of the senses (including mind) is not only clarified, purified, and emptied, it is suspended. The senses function during daily activities. In sustained zazen also, the senses are completely open – yet held in check, so to speak. As the technical Buddhist expression puts it, there is no "outflow" [Sanskrit: *âsrava*; Pali: *âsava*] – or inflow. Now we are ready for the third picture.

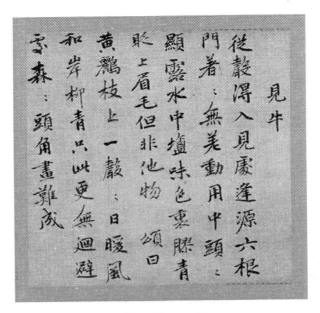

3. Finding Ox

By listening, an entrance found;
Seeing through, the source encountered.
It is this way with all six senses,
Every act crystal clear.
Like salt in water,
Or glue in paint.
Open your eye:
There's nothing else.

Nightingale singing, singing in the treetops.
Warm sun, soft breeze, riverbank willows green.
Right here, nowhere to run, nowhere to hide.
Majestic head and horns no artist could capture.

The first line harks back to picture two and gaining a foothold through such things as hearing the teachings. In early Buddhism, hearing the *Dhamma* [Sanskrit: *Dharma*], considering it, and practicing it were called the three wise ways. In ancient times, the Dharma was not written down but was orally recited and memorized. Thus, hearing it was the natural first step. In time, reading became more common, so we don't need to cling to the auditory sense. Actually, the entrance is everywhere, filling all our senses, if only we are in tune, in accord. The sustained effort of gathering all into one culminates in realizing all **is** one. Now, where does **that** come from?

Look at the picture: for the first time the ox has appeared. With the second line, we plunge right in. This is no longer catching sight of discrete tracks or hearing something in the distance. This is entering the source itself; it's "here" without a doubt. Not a sound, sight or insight, but the root-source of experience. This is not a discrete experience, however wondrous it may be, that self can have.

The third and fourth lines make clear that encountering the root-source transforms all of the senses: seeing, hearing, smelling, tasting, touching, and mind are now clear and unhindered in their functioning. The rest of the first verse reveals that all is now inseparable from the source itself: salt in water, the glue in paint suggest that the source is there "in" each and every thing, but inseparable. The source is not simply something else, something other.

Poet-layman Su Dongpo of eleventh century China expressed it as: "Gurgling brook the gold, broad tongue; are mountain colors not the pure body?" [See *ZS* 512.] Every sound, the eloquence of Buddha; every form, the body awakening.

The four-line poem for picture three sings and portrays that which is beyond sound and sight. The source is apparent wherever we look, whatever we hear or think or feel: *"rocking in the treetops, all the day long," "nowhere to run to, nowhere to hide."*

The last line of the four-line poem suggests that, although it is fully expressed in – *as* – each and every thing, the source is inexhaustible. That which you have sincerely sought and faithfully followed draws you in and shows the way. The living source that cannot be objectified or separated out – **but which you now know you are inseparable from** – will not lead you astray. Only **you** can do that. Like gravity inevitably drawing you in: resist and you're left sucked into the vacant center of your "self" instead of being drawn inevitably into the source of all.

After the Edo Period Zen master Hakuin Ekaku [白隠慧鶴 1686-1769] had his first sight of the ox, he was asked about *"Mu"* or emptiness. He replied, "No place to lay hand or foot on that." A natural response at this stage, although we will return to it later.

We left Wagner Dodge stopped in his tracks. As important as this stopping is, it is not enough. The flames still approach. There is one more thing Wagner Dodge did. It seemed so bizarre that most of the others in his crew thought he had gone crazy, so they continued running. As a result, they died. After he stopped, what did he do?

He lit a match. Burning the grass around him, he then lay down in the burned patch and escaped unscathed.

We are not fire fighters. But we, also, stop running. And instead enter the flames.

In religious practice, what remains, what survives, after all has been consumed? Put the other way around: when one has become disenchanted and dispassionate with all, who realizes release, for whom does the flame become extinguished? Only after all has been consumed can this really be known. It is now time to turn to picture four.

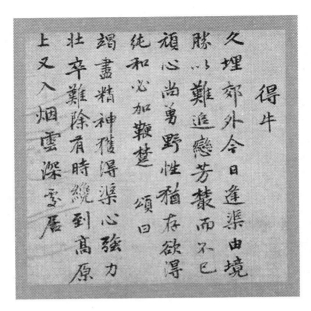

4. Catching Ox

Long hidden in wilderness,
Today finally found.
Yet hard to keep up with it wandering off:
Longing for meadows of sweet grass,
Refusing to be broken,
Wild as ever.
To bring into complete accord,
Lay on the whip!

Putting all energy into it, grab the beast.
Yet so strong and stubborn, won't be broken.
Now taking the high ground.
Now descending into misty depths.

If the ox is our so-called true self, the absolute, Buddha nature, why must it be broken and tamed?

At any rate, **you need to be firm here.** Don't ease up. As it's said: "The further you go, the deeper it gets; the more you realize, the harder you must strive." [See *ET* 17; *HP* 33, 204.] With your whole being, grab the bull by the horns and don't let go!

As the picture shows, the two are not yet completely one. But they **are** inseparable now. Be careful when discord arises; do not fall back into old ways. As the last two lines of the second verse suggest, one moment you will be taken to the very summit, the next plunged into the very depths.

Constant practice of right effort, with great trust, is required here. To really grab the bull by the horns with your whole being, you must let go of all of your

18

hopes and expectations, all of your experiences, knowledge, and insight. Such things prevent complete accord. You can't have this on **your own terms**. Simply continue on, without desire or complaint.

Remember Hakuin? Asked by the master about "*Mu*," he proudly responded: "No place to lay hand or foot on that." A fine answer, clearly displaying the young Hakuin's spiritual prowess and freedom. The master, however, exposed the place where Hakuin was still bound to his freedom by promptly squeezing Hakuin's nose and declaring, "Got a pretty good hand on it here." Then with a hearty laugh, the master spat out: "You poor hole-dwelling devil!" [See *ZMH* 118-119; *WI* 30-32; *HP* 31, 169.]

Indeed. If any such place remains in you, don't wait for me to smash it. Don't get attached to it, don't dwell or abide in it. Don't turn it into an experience you have attained: "... man must be so poor that he is not and has no place wherein God could act. Where man still preserves some place in himself, he preserves distinction. This is why I pray God to rid me of God ..." [*WJ* 214] Meister Eckhart. Don't get caught by the bull of your experience, however subtle or profound.

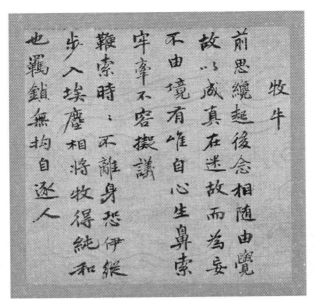

5. Taming Ox

Once a thought arises,
Another surely follows.
Wake up and all becomes truth,
Abide in ignorance and all is false.
This is not due to external conditions,
It arises from mind.
Hold tight the rope,
Do not waver.

Don't let go the whip and tether even a moment,
Or alas, the beast may wander into worldly dust.
Properly tend till tame and gentle,
Without entangling bridle, following its own accord.

As the picture shows, they now move as one. There is little resistance anymore. The going is smooth.

However, the text warns of remaining dangers. Having come this far, you might wonder how there could still be obstructions. To the question: "But after kenshō is attained and you have entered the path of enlightenment, surely there's no evil to obstruct you then?" Hakuin answers: "Indeed there is! It exists if you create it. If you don't create it, it doesn't exist. But such distinctions can wait until after you've attained the Way. You can pose such questions to yourself then – it won't be too late." [*WI* 38]

A stubborn illness requires bitter medicine. So the text for picture four stated: "To bring into complete accord, lay on the whip!" Here the tone is a bit different: "Hold tight the rope, do not waver." The text here concludes: by proper tending, it follows of its own accord, with no more need for implements or prodding.

Here, it is confirmed that this "practice" is not something you **do** at times (for example, on the zazen cushion). It is constant, it is what you **are**. Still, you must take great care not to sully or defile it.

We are now halfway through the journey. You have gotten a sense of the "process," skillfully but artificially broken up here to help us on the Way. I trust you now see that there are not really ten discrete steps or stages. Zen is not preoccupied with process or even transformation. Don't get hung up with this portrayal of the stages or the accompanying narrative. Everyone must **go through themselves**; no two paths will be the same. These depictions and descriptions can be helpful signposts and warn us of traps along the Way. The point, however, is to actually complete the journey.

Each one must make the journey themselves, but as a group practicing together, let us all continue on the Way, supporting each other and being supported by each other, determined but patient, through day and night, pleasant and unpleasant, bearable and unbearable, illusion and enlightenment. Don't stop halfway.

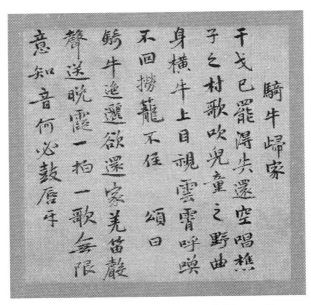

6. Returning Home Riding Ox

The struggle is over;
Loss-gain vanished.
Humming rustic tunes,
Playing a child's ditty.
Astride the ox,
Gazing at boundless sky.
Even if called, won't turn round,
Though enticed, will not stop.

Astride ox, leisurely wending the way home.
The tune dissolves evening glow.
Sentiment unbound in each beat and verse.
In tune with each other – need it be said?

With this sixth picture, the struggle has ended. The *dis-eased* subject is no more. Boundless child playing boundless tunes astride boundless ox gazing at boundless sky. This is perhaps the most famous of the oxherding pictures, similar to Daoist depictions of Lao-zi (Lao Tzu) riding off into the mountains astride an ox.

Picture and verse express a profound samadhi-at-play, or joyful samadhi, free of self-other. No need for complex philosophies, a simple song says it all:

Mr. Bluebird's on my shoulder;
It's the truth, it's actual –
Everything is satis-factual!
["Zip-A-Dee-Doo-Dah" lyrics by
Ray Gilbert, *Song of the South*, 1946]

Not a worry in the world. Who needs outside confirmation, lineage, or transmission?

Constant practice of right effort reaches fruition in effortlessness. *Dao De Jing* (*Tao Te Ching*; chapter 48) and *Zhuangzi* (*Chuang Tzu*; chapter 22) speak of "Doing nothing – yet nothing is left undone." Nothing **is** easy. This is really **running on empty**. In the beginning, each path led to a dead end; now, every road leads home.

Who is in tune with whom? As the end of the text for picture six suggests, to those who are truly intimate, what words are necessary, what praise possible? The Tang Dynasty monk Linji [Rinzai 臨濟 d. 867], the father of Rinzai Zen, demands, "Speak, speak!" [*RL* 5] He is not asking for words.

"Returning Home Riding Ox" is a marvelous moment on the Way. But there is still a ways to go.

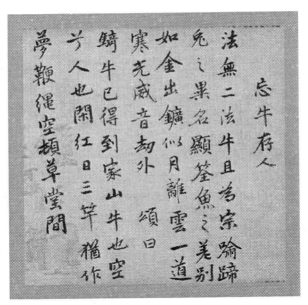

7. Ox Forgotten, Man Remains

There are not two Dharmas,
And the ox is symbolic.
The trap is left when the rabbit is snared,
The net abandoned once fish are caught.
Like gold from dross,
Or moon emerging from clouds:
The single beam shines
Prior to the world arising.

Astride the ox, the hills of home at last.
Ox vanished, you're at ease.
Sun already high in the sky, yet dream on.
Rope and whip idly lie under thatched roof.

The ox is gone – **again!** But unlike in the first (and second) picture, now there is no need to search for it. It will not reappear; even its troublesome tracks have vanished. **No bull** – another marvelous moment on the Way.

The person remains – yet he is not the child that began the journey. This **"one"** is inseparable from all. The picture shows him spontaneously bowing and putting hands together in grateful prayer. You might ask to whom or to what? But once we get here, the question answers itself; such bowing **is** the answer. Still, there is value in sincerely asking.

As the text reveals, here there are not dual Dharmas: no conflicting truths, no levels of reality. There's not really **one** either.

Separating gold from dross, moon emerging from clouds, suggests that what we desperately sought has always been here – but must be realized. The ox never

30

has gone astray – once we actually stand here, that truth is manifest. And so the ox, having done its work, is gone.

The single beam that is shining refers not only to the moon's enlightening glow; if it did, how is it prior to the world arising?

Sun already high in the sky, yet dreaming on: the peaceful slumber of awakening. Consider: "*Samsara* as well as Nirvana – like last night's dream." [See *ZMH* 39; *HP* 122, 271.] Or the Daoist expression "Sleep without dream and wake without care." [*WT* 8] Can you even remember the first picture, in which you couldn't find a moment's rest?

The implements you had used to tame and train are now idle, as trap and net are left once the creature is caught. The ways and means must be mastered – then abandoned. Don't let ways get in the way, don't turn the practice into the service of the self: "Whoever is seeking God by ways is finding ways and losing God, who in ways is hidden." [*ME* 11] Meister Eckhart. Amen.

What remains here? This alone, without object – or subject. Without *re-pre-sentation*, without being turned into something, anything, within or without: "Ox vanished, you're at ease."

But there are three more pictures – why isn't this the last one? Let us continue on and see.

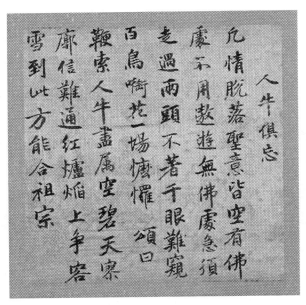

8. Man and Ox Both Forgotten

Worldly sentiment shed,
Empty even of holy intent.
Not hanging round where Buddha resides,
Quickly passing where no Buddha is.
Without abiding in either,
Not even the thousand eyes can penetrate here.
A hundred birds offering flowers –
What a shame.

Whip and rope, man and ox – all gone.
Vast azure heavens beyond reckoning.
Snowflakes can't survive flaming furnace.
Here truly one with the masters of old.

No worldly sentiment or delusion here, yet neither is there a trace of transcendent holiness, no stench of *satori*, not a whiff of enlightenment. That too must fall away. Even the falling away must fall away. How could it be any other way? Like snow falling on a hot stove, whatever flakes appear just as soon dissolve.

The thousand eyes refers to all-seeing compassionate vision. The Bodhisattva of Compassion is often represented with innumerable eyes to see and arms to aid all beings. Yet even this great being cannot **see** here. Do you see?

Although in the beginning they were spoken of separately, can you now see that the flame of self extinguished (Nirvana) and burning with compassion for others are really not two different approaches? Still wrapped up in self – or no-self – how can you really see and hear the other, let alone lend a helping hand? The immaturity of Hakuin's initial experience ("No place to lay hand or foot on that") is clear.

34

A hundred birds offering flowers refers to Niutou Farong [Gozu Hôyû 牛頭法融], a seventh-century Chinese monk who was so saintly and devoted in his practice that flocks of birds brought flowers in their beaks as offerings. When he met the Fourth Patriarch of Chinese Zen and penetrated here, they stopped the fuss.

Where is the teacher or master in all of this? Of course, you can say that you are constantly being guided, inspired, prodded, and challenged. But note well that nowhere in these pictures does a teacher appear for the "poor" oxherder. Others who have made the journey already, and companions on the way, can be of great help. But each one of us must make the journey. Again: **this, which we in all sincerity seek, shows the Way**. This is the only teacher necessary, as Gotama's own example reveals.

All of the pictures are done inside a circle, a kind of *ensô* or Zen circle. This eighth picture is just the circle, lightly shaded for effect. Like an empty mirror. What does it reflect? Nothing? Everything? Is this so-called vast emptiness, or is all really present (though not *re-presented*) for the first time? Let us enter and see.

35

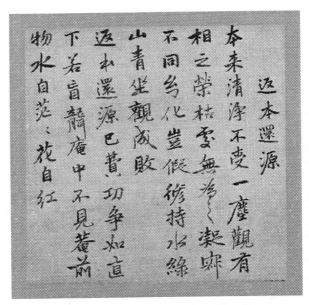

返本還源

物水下若返山本
水自若盲還青来
自茫盲聾源坐清
茫庵庵已觀净
花中中費成不
自不不功敗曾
红見見争有相不
庵前如一之同
前直塵荣為
觀枯化
有零豈
無假
為修
寂持
寞水
绿

9. Return to Origin, Back at Source

Originally pure and clean,
Without a speck of dust.
Seen through, the growth and decay of all forms.
At ease in the unconditioned.
Without illusory phantoms,
What is there to embellish?
Waters blue, mountains green.
Sit and see through the change of things.

Return to origin, back at source – what wasted effort.
Far better just to be blind and deaf.
Inside the hut, no sight of things outside.
Streams flow their own accord, roses naturally bloom red.

Every day the sun rises and sets; each moment the whole world awakens – from where, for whom?

An earlier version of Zen *Oxherding Pictures* consists of only five pictures, with the ox gradually losing its dark color and ending with the empty circle. To avoid misunderstanding mere emptiness as the end and goal, eventually one more picture was added. This sixth one is similar to the tenth and final picture here. Two verses for that sixth and final picture begin (freely rendered):

With the marvelous end one has finished dying,
yet even here there is a way through:
Back amidst the six realms [of samsaric existence:
gods, men, demigods, animals, hungry spirits, hell] …

The very root of life extinguished –
then springs to life again [literally revived or resurrected] ...

As we will see in detail in the next chapter, this extremity of Great Doubt is the Great Death spoken of in Zen Buddhism, and it culminates in the Great Awakening, or Great Rebirth. Now it's real: "Never gone astray – what need to search?" Return to the origin, back at the source? Bah, so much wasted effort! Inside the hut, no sight, no *re-presentation*, of things outside. What is outside – or inside – this? Do you see why this ninth picture is "further," "beyond" the eighth picture?

Better to be blind and deaf? Whoa, this isn't politically correct! Could it mean that reality – **this** – is perceived only when self is deprived of all six senses, bereft of all sense? Often expressed as seeing with the ears and hearing with the eyes. With this, the tenth and final picture can be discerned.

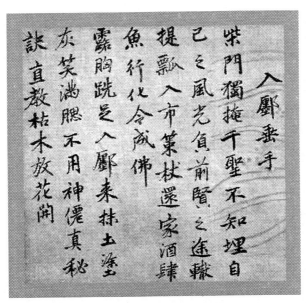

10. Entering Market with Open Hands

Alone behind brushwood door,
Not even the thousand saints know.
Hiding his light,
Not following the tracks of past sages.
Carrying his gourd, he enters the market.
Leaning on his staff, he returns home.
Hanging round honky-tonks and fish stalls,
All become Buddhas.

Entering market with bare chest and bare feet.
Smeared with mud and ash, broad face beaming.
No display of magic powers.
Yet withered trees burst into bloom.

Note that the oxherd is now a chubby Buddha aiding a young inquirer. The circle is complete – yet there is nothing remarkable here. Not a glimmer of inner experience. Covered in the mud and ash of serving others, with a look not unlike that of a fool. Not simply free **from** care, but free **to** care – no strings attached. No special powers or charisma – yet somehow all are saved. The verse for picture eight included being truly one with the masters of old; now there is no thought even to follow in such tracks.

Instead, we carry our gourd to market. We go about our daily work. Conventional commentaries mention that the gourd is a symbol of emptiness. Other commentaries mention that it was also used for carrying wine. The two complement each other well, for we continue to observe the precepts – without being intoxicated even by them.

42

Why enter such worldly and "corrupt" places? Certainly not the place for a self-respecting monastic. Not there to enjoy himself – but not there in order to save others either. Precisely because there is no such intent (secular or sacred), all are embraced and "become" Buddhas just as they are. Just like right here and now:

> *Numberless beings – set free*
> *Endless delusion – let go*
> *Countless Dharma – see through*
> *Peerless Way – manifest!*

So go our four great, or universal, vows.

As Guoan's disciple Ziyuan put it in his introduction: "Who **is** that devil at the end entering the market?" [See *TO 2.*]

NOTES

Transcript based on retreat lectures given in 2009 in Japan, the U. S., and throughout Europe. I would like to thank participants in my seminar at Hanazono University for their comments on the verse translations: Zen master-scholar Sodô Yasunaga, Zen monk-scholar Takuma Senda, Zen laywoman Takami Yoshie, Helen Findley (Fulbright scholar, University of Chicago), and Casper Wits (Japanese Ministry of Education scholar, Kyoto University).

For elephant-training pictures in the Tibetan tradition, see Geshe Rabten, *Treasury of Dharma* (Tharpa Publications, 1997) pp. 115ff.

Great Doubt:
Getting Stuck and
Breaking Through
The Real Koan

Raising my head to look about,　　　　　舉頭看見日初圓
I saw that the sun has always been round.
… And ever since then have been joyful.　　…直至如今常快活
　　　　(Luohan [Rakan羅漢; circa 866-928] *ZD* 247-48 rev.)

Ever since seeing peach blossoms,　　　　自從一見桃花後,
I have never doubted again.　　　　　　直至如今更不疑。
　　　　(Lingyun [Reiun靈雲; ninth century] *EV* 6-7 rev.)

Ever since being kicked by master Ma[zu],　自從一喫馬師踢,
I have not stopped laughing!　　　　　　直至如今笑不休。
　　　　　　　　(See *SB* 77;馬録83)

Where do such statements come from? How are they possible? This retreat
will be a chance for you to discover where – in yourself – such statements arise and
why they are not only possible but necessary.

During the retreat, I will present a short text, *Exhortations for Those Who Don't
Arouse the Doubt*, from Boshan [Hakusan 博山; 1575-1630], one of the leading
Chinese masters of the Ming Dynasty.

Doubt? Like other religions, Buddhism encourages faith, trust. Doubt – along
with greed, hatred, ignorance, and pride – is usually considered a defilement or
poison. Indeed, such doubt is to be avoided: doubt as mere skepticism, a lack of
trust, or a hesitant attitude that keeps you from entering the Way.

That is nothing like the Doubt spoken of in Zen Buddhism. There is good reason it is called **Great** Doubt. In an introductory section to his text, Boshan briefly
describes the barrier (also called the great matter) of life-and-death or birth-death,
the Doubt [疑情; literally "doubt sensation"] that arises from it, how this fundamental religious question differs from ordinary doubt and skepticism, and its final
congealing into the Doubt Block [疑團] or Great Doubt [大疑]:

In Zen practice, the essential point is to arouse Doubt. What is this Doubt?
For example, when you are born, where do you come from? You cannot
help but remain in doubt about this. When you die, where do you go?
Again, you cannot help but remain in doubt. Since you cannot pierce this
barrier of life-and-death, suddenly the Doubt will coalesce right before
your eyes. Try to put it down, you cannot; try to push it away, you cannot. Eventually this Doubt Block will be broken through and you'll realize
what a worthless notion is life-and-death – ha! As the old worthies said:
"Great Doubt, Great Awakening; small doubt, small awakening; no doubt,
no awakening."
做工夫。貴在起疑情。何謂疑情。如生不知何來。不得不疑來處。死不
知何去。不得不疑去處。生死關竅不破。則疑情頓發。結在眉睫上。放
亦不下。趁亦不去。忽朝樸破疑團。生死二字是甚麼閑家具。嗯。古德
云。大疑大悟。小疑小悟。不疑不悟。

[X 63, 756a]

47

Far from being a lack of trust or faith, Great Doubt can arise only **from** Great Trust. Great Trust grounds and supports us; Great Doubt keeps us on the path, leads us all the way through. Great Trust is the conviction, based on experience, that there is a way; Great Doubt provides the fuel to go all the way: "Fully trust, you'll fully doubt; fully doubt, you'll fully awaken." [信有十分、疑有十分。疑有十分、悟有十分。禅関 45; *T* 48, 1099a; cf. *MK* 36] This doubt is an intense wonder, a healthy curiosity that opens us. Is it not fear – a lack of trust, which is a denial of our doubt – that blinds and binds us?

But why focus on doubt – isn't Great Trust alone enough? Yes, it is! All we need to do is trust **completely**. Then, **whatever** we encounter, there can be no doubt, no hesitation. Now, who here has this kind of trust? Anyone?

You have just answered your own question. Great Trust is indeed enough. Yet as Boshan said and you just confirmed, doubt cannot be avoided. For your very self is split, within and without. To put it bluntly, you don't simply **have** this split; you **are** this split. Self comes into being split: with faith – and with doubt. **See your self**: right here, the basis of Buddhism is discovered under your feet.

Unlike ordinary doubt, which can cause wavering and a loss of focus, Great Doubt solidifies and gathers focus. The Chinese Zen layman Suan [素菴; late thirteenth century]:

> Nowadays, those who devote themselves to Zen practice are few. Once a koan is taken up, [most people] find their minds trapped by the twin demons of torpor and scattering. They don't realize that Doubt vanquishes [falling into] torpor and [mental] scattering. If Trust is firm, Doubt will be firm; once Doubt is firm, torpor and scattering will naturally vanish.
> 近來篤志參禪者少。纔參箇話頭、便被昏散二魔纏縛、不知昏散與疑情正相對治。信心重則疑情必重。疑情重則昏散自無。
> [禅関 60; T 48, 1099c; cf. *MK* 43-44]

The lecture title "Great Doubt: Getting Stuck and Breaking Through The Real Koan" refers to arousing this Great Doubt and having it resolved, once and for all. Whether such language is used or not, this can be considered the foundation, the heart, of Zen practice, and the unique – the distinctive and defining – character of Zen Buddhism. As Boshan declared: "In Zen practice, the essential point is to arouse Doubt." As we will see, this is true of both Rinzai and Sôtô Zen.

In a word, our actual doubt, this intense wonder and healthy curiosity, becomes the way through. Rather than denying it, the Zen Buddhist approach is: "So, you have doubt? Then doubt away – take that doubt all the way!" This is consummate Great Trust at work. What else do you need? Going through your own Great Doubt is the way to really put it to rest, once and for all.

Perhaps Great Doubt can be considered an essential element of any religious practice – without it, why practice? It's clearly central to Buddhism: look at the life of Gotama Buddha, his great renunciation or leaving home, his struggle and awakening. Through it all, his quest to resolve it is unmistakable.

Monk: Zen masters since of old have said that Great Awakening proceeds from Great Doubt. [literally "At the bottom of Great Doubt lies Great Awakening"大疑の下に大悟あり] You don't use this Great Doubt in your teaching. Why?

Bankei: Long ago, when Nanyue went to the sixth patriarch and was asked, "What is it that's just come?" he was totally bewildered. His Doubt about it lasted for eight long years. Finally he was able to respond, "Whatever I say would miss the mark." Now that's really Great Doubt and Great Awakening!

Suppose you lost your only surplice, the one you were given when you became a monk, and you were unable to find it no matter how hard you looked. You'd search and search without letup. You'd be unable to stop searching for even an instant. That would be real doubt!

People nowadays say they need to have doubt because people in the past did. So they cultivate a doubt. But that's merely an imitation of a doubt, not a real one, so the day never comes when they arrive at a real resolution. It's as if you were to go off looking for something you hadn't really lost, pretending you had.

[*UB* 129-30 rev.; 盤珪137]

Japanese Zen master Bankei [盤珪1622-93] is not criticizing Great Doubt – he himself was spurred on by it since childhood. He **is** criticizing unnatural, forced, contrived, made-up doubt based on someone else's words or experience. Bankei is right.

Bankei mentions the story of Nanyue's [Nangaku南嶽; 677-744] encounter with the sixth patriarch of Chinese Zen. (Nanyue is pivotal in Zen Buddhism as a disciple of the sixth patriarch and as the teacher of Mazu [Baso馬祖; 709-788].) When asked where he had come from, Nanyue responded: "From Mount Song." Then the sixth patriarch challenged: "What is it that's just come?"[什麼物恁麼來] This served as the catalyst for Nanyue's Great Doubt. (See *EV* 62.)

Once you recognize this great matter of life-and-death under your own feet, Great Doubt is not far behind. Otherwise, Zen practice stagnates and various problems arise. Although formally sitting in meditation, mind goes round and round the same old circles or becomes attached to states of stillness, clarity, and so on. It has always been so. It was so 300 or 400 years ago in China and Japan: as we will see, Boshan described it in his work *Exhortations for Those Who Don't Arouse the Doubt*, as did Bankei, and many others. Failure to realize one's own Great Doubt continues today in Zen groups around the world. I trust that you see the significance of our theme and will forgive me for stubbornly focusing on it. It is **just what is needed**.

What is this Great Doubt? First of all, as Bankei just made clear, it's not something you have to create, think up – or be given. Great Doubt is the most natural thing in this world.

Frankly, I wonder how you avoid it. Stop running from it and it's manifest;

49

open your eye and it can't be avoided, as Boshan suggested. At first, it may feel like a bowling ball in the pit of your stomach.

In the beginning, I quoted a Zen monk who sang in his enlightenment poem of "*Raising my head to look about, I saw that the sun has always been round. … And ever since then have been joyful.*" Earlier in that very poem, he stated clearly where he was before awakening:

> *The Doubt Block within me*   心裏癡[疑]團若栲栳
> *like a large wicker basket.*

Great Doubt can arise anytime, anywhere – if we let it: "*I just don't know what to do with myself.*" Dionne Warwick and Dusty Springfield sang this Burt Bacharach-Hal David hit when I was growing up in the mid-1960s. You know how to do all kinds of things, don't you? **Do you know what to do with your self?**

What drives some to work themselves to the bone while others try and shirk as much work as possible? What drives some to seek more and more material comfort while others are driven to give up all they have? What drives some into relationships that they then destroy while others refuse to have real relationships at all? Could any of this be a reaction to that doubt, or perhaps a desperate escape from it? What is that boundless quandary that wells up in all of us on occasion, despite – or in light of – our apparent firm grasp of our self and our situation? Always just out of reach, yet never far away. What if we no longer push it away but instead embrace it with an open heart and mind?

There are as many entrances to Great Doubt as there are people. Simply inquire into what's under your own feet, at the heart of it all. What's there? Realizing this is what zazen meditation is all about. What drives us to love others – yet keeps us separate from them, keeps us from loving fully? Who is this one that comes to life precariously poised between life-and-death? Here is the great matter of life-and-death, the only real koan there is.

More concretely: this doubt might first arise as a kind of intuition. It comes down to the fact that **I don't know** – who I am, where I come from, what is real, and so on.

Or it may first arise as a deep-seated sensation, emotion, or feeling. It comes down to feeling **I'm not at peace**, I cannot come fully to rest with myself or with others; something's not right.

Or it may first arise as a problem of will[1] or volition. I sense that, no matter what, **I can't seem to get free**, as if I'm banging up against the wall of myself. For example, however much I try to do what is good and right, I fail.

However it may first arise, it's essential to properly direct and focus the doubt. Otherwise, the doubt may be clear and solidify for a while, but then it fades again into the background. It remains inconclusive, indecisive. It will never be fully resolved that way. It needs to come to its own end, its own conclusion. This is the function of a real koan and the value of working with authentic guides who have gone through it themselves.

Zen masters such as Dahui [Daie 大慧; 1089-1163], who championed sustained koan introspection or koan inquiry to arouse Great Doubt, speak of "The thousand doubts, the ten thousand doubts – just One [Great] Doubt." [千疑万疑只是一疑] Such statements are easy to misunderstand. From the outside, it may sound like taking that wicker basket and filling it with all of your doubts. You will never arrive at the Great Doubt that way. The direction is into the source of your actual doubt rather than out to an endless increase or proliferation of possible doubts. There is nothing more concrete and immediate, more pressing and urgent, more total and all-encompassing than this Great Doubt. Eventually, you are the Great Doubt, and the Great Doubt is you. In this light, our ordinary doubts are quite abstract, aren't they?

In sustained practice, allow yourself to settle into this Doubt, this **genuine hunger**, rather than escape into false hungers and phony satisfactions. If it first arises as a kind of intuition – that you do not know – then inquire with your whole being: Who is it? What is it? The Hindu sage Ramana Maharshi (1879-1950) used the question "Who am I?" To return to Boshan: who comes into being at birth, who dies at death? Better yet: right now who is reading this? Who is actually behind it all? Unless that's clear, nothing is clear, is it? For Bankei, this question naturally arose from childhood in terms of what, where, is my intrinsic, bright virtue [明德]? The sixth patriarch challenged with the question: "What is it that's just come?" In more traditional Zen terms, "What is your original face?" Or "All things return to one; where does this one return to?" Whatever form it takes, the point is for the question to come to encompass all – beginning with oneself.

If it first arises more as a feeling – that you are not at peace – then inquire directly into who it is that is not at peace. This challenge was the beginning of the Zen tradition in China. (See *ZCM*, case 41.) Another way of expressing it: "How can I avoid cold and heat?" As a koan, the question is not just about coolness and warmth but rather the entire dualistic complex that self is trapped in. Another way of expressing it: "I am so poor. Master, please enrich me." The questioner was not begging for material wealth – he was a homeless monk. (These last two questions, by the way, were asked of the co-founders of the Sôtô Zen tradition. Their superb answers continue inspiring us to this day.)

If it first arises more as a problem of will, see into Shitou's [Sekitô 石頭; 700-791] challenge: "As you are will not do; not as you are will not do. Either way, nothing will do. Now what?" [恁麼也不得。不恁麼也不得。恁麼不恁麼總不得。子作麼生。Cf. 馬録107-08; *X* 69, 5a; *SB* 81] In more traditional Zen terms, "Both speech and silence are relative; how can we be free?" Again, the question must come to include the whole dualistic complex that self is, not just the matter of speech or silence. More simply, see into the question: "Right here and now, what is lacking?"

Don't have time for such Doubt? How much of your life – and your practice – is spent avoiding, denying it? Genuine Zen practice naturally awakens, fosters, encourages this Doubt and helps you pour yourself completely into it so that it can be truly resolved once and for all. Nothing strange or unnatural. Look and see: after all, Great Doubt is what self really is. **Not** inquiring into this is what is really strange and unnatural, isn't it? Thus your lingering discontent, your hunger that cannot be assuaged no matter how many relationships you go into and out of. Thus your misplaced pride about how many years you've sat zazen or how many koans you've passed. This Doubt is the precious gift each one of us was given upon entering the world. Unwrap it and see your self!

Great Doubt cannot be an object of awareness; it is much more real and immediate than that. As a mere object of awareness, it degenerates into endless speculative questions **about** it – what Bankei and others warned against. **Let it be what it really is.** No need to contrive, don't get "caught in another man's tub," as Bankei put it (*UB* 133).

As we will see in *Exhortations for Those Who Don't Arouse the Doubt*, Boshan repeatedly drives home the fact that if Great Doubt is not allowed to arise, Zen practice sinks into an unhealthy "sickness." An escape into calm and clear mind states, insights, so-called enlightenment experiences that self assumes will solve all its problems – all the while leaving the fundamental self-delusion untouched. See for yourself: such states and experiences are a part of the *dis-ease*. Open yourself up to your own Great Doubt and you can avoid such problems. There's no room for such delusions here.

Now, how do you actually arouse Great Doubt? Zazen meditation is a most helpful entrance. In sustained zazen, gather all your energy into one. [*Demonstrates*]

This is a samadhi or concentrated oneness that's completely natural, calm, attentive, and focused, yet open. It is a constant energy that nothing can stop. Thus the value of sustained zazen and a retreat like this. Ego-self's endless escapades, escapes, vicious cycles are rendered powerless, at least for now. Be aware if they return.

In Japanese Sôtô Zen, the focus is spoken of as untainted, uncontrived "just sitting," *shikan-taza* [只管打坐]. Not mere sitting in blankness or clarity. Dôgen [道元 1200-1253], the father of Japanese Sôtô Zen, struggled with this Doubt since his youth and had it resolved through a decisive awakening he described as "body-mind fallen off," *shinjin-datsuraku* [身心脱落]. He even states in his work, *Bendôwa* [辨道話]: "With this, the one great matter of my entire life was resolved" [一生参学の大事ここにをはりぬ]. Where is Sôtô Zen today?

Just sitting **is** enough – **if it is thoroughgoing**. There can be no thought of doubt, let alone awakening. Sitting itself **is** Great Doubt Awakening, the *genjô-kôan* or manifest koan. [*Demonstrates*] Do you see how pure, how simple – and how difficult, how uncompromising – just sitting really is? By the way, Boshan, who focused in his *Exhortations* on the necessity of arousing this Doubt, was one of the leading Sôtô [Ts'ao-tung 曹洞] masters of Ming China.

Whether just sitting or working with a koan, **all** is naturally fused into one. [*Demonstrates:*] One... concrete... whole. In this way, the entire self-complex, what Dôgen called body-mind, naturally becomes stuck (as the title of this lecture suggests). Frozen. All comes to a stop – in a most sublime, marvelous manner. Hakuin, the reviver of Rinzai Zen in Japan, described it: "Like sitting in an ice cave ten thousand miles thick." [*ZCM* 289 rev.; cf. *HP* 25; *ZMH* 118; 遠羅 118] In traditional Buddhist terms, there is no "outflow" – or inflow. Yet everything is there – **crystal clear** – in a manner impossible for ordinary consciousness. For it is not objectified, not turned into something as an object of consciousness. Here is the entrance to realized Zen practice, to body-mind **fallen off**. A moment ago, I asked where Sôtô Zen is today; the same must be asked of Rinzai Zen.

Echoing the Sôtô master Boshan's introductory remarks, Rinzai master Hakuin said:

> To all intents and purposes, Zen practice makes as its essential the resolu-
> tion of the Doubt Block. Thus it is said, "At the bottom of Great Doubt
> lies Great Awakening. If you doubt fully you will awaken fully." [大疑ノ下
> 二大悟アリ、疑ガヒ十分アレバ悟リ十分有リト。]
>
> [*ZMH* 144 rev.; 遠羅489]

Once Great Doubt is aroused and maintained, there is little danger of abid-ing in static oneness or of getting attached to mystic experiences. The resolution of this Great Doubt is not a matter of **self breaking into** and abiding in a state of oneness or of **self breaking out of** limits such as space and time. Rather, **the very doubt-separation that self is, is broken through**. This is body-mind fallen off. The separation and doubt that self is, are gone! This is where genuine love arises. This is where genuine Zen statements, including the ones I opened with, naturally arise. And where another kind of practice naturally begins.

Don't sit there waiting for something to happen. Such practice is criticized as "awaiting-enlightenment" [待悟]. If you're waiting for something, you're not giv-ing yourself fully to practice, are you? You're actually abiding in a state of ignorance, "binding yourself without a rope" [無繩自縛; see *RL* 139].

Give yourself in all sincerity, then you can't help but realize this Doubt. Don't waste time thinking: "Maybe I don't have that kind of doubt, I need more doubt, I need his doubt." Simply remain open to what's in your own heart, under your own feet. Don't avoid it; instead, embrace it. That's all you need.

What about this Doubt in ordinary life, in relations with others – won't it in-terfere? If it's real, you will find it's **just what is needed**. Relations with others are transformed: embracing and seeing through our own doubt, we can truly open up, make room for and respond to the real need of the other. We can love the other for who they really are – not for what we need them to be. At peace ourselves, we can truly be with others, supporting and being supported by them. See for yourself.

To sum up: naturally rouse this Great Doubt with your own living koan or a traditional koan. After all, koan and doubt are not two separate things:

Question: Practicing under teachers, some of them say to focus on the koan and some say to doubt the koan. Are these the same or different?
Answer: As soon as you focus on the koan, doubt arises – why separate them? [They are the same.] Focus on the koan and doubt will immedi-ately arise. Continue investigating, and when your efforts reach their limit,

you'll naturally awaken.

問。學人參求知識。或令提箇話頭。或令疑箇話頭。同耶別耶。答。纔舉
話頭。當下便疑。豈有二理。一念提起。疑情即現。覆去翻來精研推究。
功深力極。自得了悟。

[*Cf.* 禅関 146; *T* 48, 1105a; *MK* 82]

Just sitting itself can be your *genjô-kôan*, the manifest koan. Then during one-on-one, we can see what's what.

Or if right now you're in great pain, then that'll do — **just don't separate from it**. Instead, enter it: who is suffering? Right there is the end of the self that suffers.

Rejoice! Where you are right now is right where you need to be. You couldn't be in a better situation. You don't need another thing. As mentioned before, someone struggling with this long ago in China once begged: "I am so poor; master, please enrich me." What was the response? The master called out the monk's name. The monk replied: "Yes?" The master responded: "You've just had three glasses of vintage Chateau Margaux — how can you say your lips are dry?"

Okay, maybe I revised that last quote about rice wine a bit. But I trust you get the point. Now dive in and taste it yourself!

Retreat Lectures

In the introductory lecture, we looked into the Great Doubt and how to arouse it. Just as Boshan, Bankei, and others responded to their situations, we must do the same. Finding Boshan's *Exhortations for Those Who Don't Arouse the Doubt* most appropriate, I present it here. The preface written by a lay disciple in 1611 states it is "truly a lifeboat for this degenerate age, a direct path for beginner's mind. Surely beneficial in the present day, it will be a great aid in the future as well." [正末世舟杭。初心徑路。豈但有益於今日。亦有補於將來。 *X* 63, 755b] If Boshan's *Exhortations* speak to you, take them to heart. If not, then just continue your practice.

In an introductory section already quoted, Boshan briefly described this Doubt. Given the practice in Zen circles nowadays, it bears repeating. The first sentence alone is priceless:

> In Zen practice, the essential point is to arouse Doubt. What is this Doubt? For example, when you are born, where do you come from? You cannot help but remain in doubt about this. When you die, where do you go? Again, you cannot help but remain in doubt. Since you cannot pierce this barrier of life-and-death, suddenly the Doubt will coalesce right before your eyes. Try to put it down, you cannot; try to push it away, you cannot. Eventually this Doubt Block will be broken through and you'll realize what a worthless notion is life-and-death – ha! As the old worthies said: "Great Doubt, Great Awakening; small doubt, small awakening; no doubt, no awakening."

Boshan and others such as Hanshan [Kanzan 憨山;1546-1623; see *PZ* 85-6] emphasize two main entrances to this Doubt: not knowing where we came from at birth and where we will go to at death.

Once we open up, however, we realize that we don't really know **anything** – we don't even know where we really are right now. **Here** Great Doubt manifests.

Otherwise, you may be preoccupied only with the first and last moments of birth and death or get lost in morbid notions of past or future lives, heaven and hell, and so on. Start where you actually are, with your present experience – not some concept or theory or someone else's words or experience. Then you won't go astray.

Boshan does not go into detail here, but the doubt at first may be vague and unfocused. No problem. With all the wonder and curiosity that you have, open up to the fact that you don't know. In proper and sustained zazen, let this doubt clearly manifest. Driven by the genuine need to know, calmly but constantly inquire. Proceed so that this doubt encompasses all. When this comes to a head, it congeals, solidifies into the Doubt Block [疑團], also called the Great Doubt Block [大疑團] or simply Great Doubt [大疑]. This, broken through, is Great Awakening, body-mind fallen off.

Developing powers of calm and clear observation, of single-minded concentration, and of direct perception (without discursive thought) can be most helpful. In the Great Doubt Block, however, all activities of consciousness have come to a halt. Hakuin often described his own experience: "All the workings of mind – thought, consciousness, emotions – hung suspended" (*RAH* 250). "Ordinary mental processes, consciousness, and emotions all ceased to function" (*HP* 25). At this point, simply continue on in Great Trust to the very end.

Such may suffice as a brief "blueprint" for arousing and breaking through the Great Doubt. Now forget all such distinctions and dive right in!

In India and China, in the past and the present, of all the worthies who spread this light, none did anything more than simply resolve this one Doubt. The thousand doubts, the ten thousand doubts are just this one Doubt. Resolve this Doubt and no doubt remains.

西天此土。古今知識。發揚此段光明。莫不只是一箇決疑而已。千疑萬疑。只是一疑。決此疑者。更無餘疑。

[Gaofeng Yuanmiao 高峰原妙; 1238-1295 in *BUS* 373 rev.; *X* 70, 707a]

This Doubt is another name for what is most pressing and urgent. Once you acknowledge this pressing and urgent matter of life-and-death as your own, the Doubt will arise of its own accord. If you continue to doubt, then quite naturally the time and conditions will arrive. If you idle away your time without making efforts and merely wait for enlightenment, the day will never come.

疑之一字。切之別名耳。總是生死心切。便自起疑。疑來疑去。自然有箇時節。若泛泛過日。不實用心。待他自[日?]悟。決無此理。

[Zongbao 宗寶; 1600-1661; Boshan Dharma heir, in *X* 72, 743b]

It is all a matter of raising or failing to raise this Doubt Block. It must be understood that this Doubt Block is like a pair of wings that advances you along the way.

[Hakuin in *ZMH* 146 rev.; 遠羅 157]

Exhortations For Those
Who Don't Arouse The Doubt

By the Chinese Master Boshan (1575-1630)
博山和尚參禪警語卷下 示疑情發不起警語
[Numbers and Titles for the ten sections have been provided.]

1. The Disease of Intellect

If you're unable to arouse the Doubt when practicing Zen, you may seek intellectual understanding through the written word. Stringing together with a single thread the various phrases and teachings of Buddhas and patriarchs, you stamp them all with one seal. If a koan [公案] is brought up, you are quick to give your interpretation. Unable to arouse your own Doubt concerning the koan [話頭], you don't like it when someone probes you with serious questions. All this is simply your wavering mind [生滅心]; it is not Zen.

You may respond at once to questions by raising a finger or showing a fist. Taking up ink brush, you promptly pen a verse to show off, hoping to guide [參究] unwitting students to your level. Fascinated with all this, you refer to it as the gate of enlightenment. You don't realize that such karmic consciousness [識心] is precisely what prevents this Doubt from arising. If only you would straight off see the error of your ways, then you should once and for all let go of all and seek out a good teacher or Dharma friend [善知識] to help you find an entrance. If not, your wavering mind will prevail, you'll become as if demon-possessed, and release will be very difficult.

Commentary

The exact circumstances under which Boshan presented these *Exhortations* are unclear. The point, however, is what they say to us here and now.

It is quite natural for Boshan to begin with the problem of mistaking mere intellectual understanding for realization. Who here has not made that mistake? The term "wavering mind," which appears at the end of the first paragraph and which he repeats often, is literally "arising-ceasing mind" [生滅心]: the restless, *samsaric* mind of life-and-death. In the present context, instead of putting the wavering mind to rest, you end up using it to spin intellectual interpretations, a subtle sleight of hand to veil the precipitous doubt underfoot.

The second paragraph points out the foolish imitation that results: raising a finger (see *ZCM* case three) or fist, composing Zen-like poetry without having resolved the great matter, and so on. In some Zen circles nowadays, declaring "Don't know!" has become the same kind of blind imitation – mouthing someone else's words in a way that actually prevents real doubt from arising. As we will see, Boshan repeatedly condemns such "performance Zen." Another critic in the late Ming Dynasty, the scholar Qian Qianyi [錢謙益; 1582-1664], stated:

Present-day Chan [Zen] is not Chan. It is no more than beating and shouting... The demonstration in the Dharma hall is like actors ascending the stage; paying homage and offering certification of enlightenment are similar to a drama acted out by little boys… They boast to each other about the number of their followers, the extent of their fame, and the wealth of their profits and patronage.

[ED 159-60 rev.]

Any better today? Let go of everything you've accumulated over the years, all the pop-Zen you've read, your intellectual understanding, and so on and honestly recognize: I don't **really** know anything. One drop of **this** is better than a truckload of someone else's garbage – especially mine! [*Laughter*]

Is your zazen firmly established, or is it still something your wavering mind goes into and out of? Are you still detoured from your Doubt by intellectual sleight of hand? Be patient, but not lax, properly focused on the matter at hand.

Inquire in all sincerity. Look at the opening of that enlightenment poem about the sun having always been round – how different is it from your own situation?

Around the seventh year of Xiantong era [circa 866]	咸通七載初参道
[I was born and soon] began to inquire into the Way.	
Wherever I went I met with words	到處逢言不識言
but couldn't understand them.	
The Doubt Block within me	心裏癡團若栲栳
like a large wicker basket.	
For three springs [years] I found no joy	三春不樂止林泉
even stopping among wooded streams…	

Did the author pontificate about the words and phrases, the koans and commentaries he met with everywhere? He recognized he couldn't really understand them. Thus, he sincerely searched and was eventually able to have a genuine Dharma encounter, which he details in his poem, climaxing in:

… My Doubt Block shattered	駭散癡團獦狙落
and fell with a crash!	
Raising my head to look about	舉頭看見日初圓
I saw that the sun has always been round.	
After that I went wandering –	從茲蹭蹬以碨碨
clump-clump, clack-clack.	
And ever since then	直至如今常快活
have been joyful.	
Belly now full	只聞肚裏飽膨脝
having eaten my fill.	
I no longer go in search	更不東西去持鉢
begging bowl in hand.	

[ZD 247-8 rev.; T 51, 288c]

The author of this poem was Luohan [Rakan羅漢; circa 866-928]. His disciple Fayan [Hôgen 法眼; 885-958] became founder of the Zen school that bears his name. When they met at Luohan's monastery, he asked Fayan why he was not out on pilgrimage. Fayan: "I don't know." The master: "Not knowing is most intimate!" [不知最親切] With this, Fayan broke through.

Don't be afraid of really not knowing! It is the entrance. But don't dwell in it either. This is the theme of the second section.

2. The Disease of Quiet Meditation

If you're unable to arouse the Doubt when practicing Zen, you may develop an aversion to the world of conditions. Thus, you escape to a quiet place and sink into zazen meditation. Empowered by this, you find it quite fascinating. When you have to get up and do something, however, you dislike it. This too is simply your wavering mind; it is not Zen.

Sitting long in zazen, sunk in quietness; within this mystic darkness the senses fuse, objects and opposition disappear. But even if you enter *dhyâna*-absorption [禪定] without mind movement, it's no different from the Hinayana [小乗: "small vehicle" of self-enlightenment]. Any contact with the world and you feel uneasy with your loss of freedom: hearing sounds or seeing sights, you're gripped by fear. Frightened, you become as if demon-possessed and commit evil acts. In the end, you waste a lifetime of practice in vain. All because from the first, you failed to arouse this Doubt – thus, you did not seek out a true guide or trust one. Instead, you stubbornly sit self-satisfied in your quiet hole. Even if you meet a good teacher or Dharma friend, if you don't immediately recognize your error, innumerable Buddhas may appear and preach the Dharma but they won't be able to save you.

Commentary

In this second section, Boshan turns to the disease of (attachment to) quiet meditation. If you think you've gotten beyond the disease of intellectual entanglement mentioned in section one, then this will likely shake you from your slumber.

The crux of this section (and the following two sections) warns against seeking shelter from the storm in the apparently peaceful cave of dead stillness. Is your zazen an escape from problems, within or without? Such is not Zen; it is the death of Zen. Great Doubt is not a matter of blotting out our actual problems; it opens us up to them, even as it directs us to their source.

Boshan speaks ill of "Hinayana" attainment. This derogatory term is often used in Zen to refer to **anyone** attached to self-serving states. It is not a sectarian criticism of non-"Mahayana" ("great vehicle" which saves all) schools of Buddhism. Still, Boshan cannot escape criticism here. I trust he will humbly bow to political correctness.

At any rate, the precious point he makes is that even such profound meditative states can be tempting escapes. Beware! As mentioned in the introductory lecture, genuine "just sitting" is enough – **if it goes all the way.**

If it doesn't, you may end up losing your temper when something intrudes on the peaceful state you cultivated while sitting. Far from peaceful, your wavering mind ends up more frightened and frustrated than before, becoming what Boshan called demon-possessed. If you are honest with yourself, how can genuine doubt **not** arise?

In my introductory comments, I mentioned a brief blueprint for breaking through the Great Doubt. Although it may be useful, it is just a blueprint. What actually arises in your practice? Present **that** in one-on-one – not what you **think** should arise. Otherwise, you are likely covering over concerns that are there and need to be acknowledged. This leads to the third section.

3. The Disease of Suppression

If you're unable to arouse the Doubt when practicing Zen, you may suppress emotions and discriminating consciousness so that no delusions can arise, then dwell in this apparently calm and lucid state. But you fail to thoroughly break through the root-source of consciousness and instead dwell on its immaculateness. Even though you may practice and understand everything from within this apparently pure and lucid state, once you encounter someone who points out your failure, then emotions and discriminating consciousness pop up like a gourd that was pushed under water. This too is simply your wavering mind; it is not Zen.

And all because from the time you first took up a koan you failed to arouse this Doubt. Even if you could suppress all delusions so that they no longer arise, it would be like trying to press down the grass with a stone [delusions will just grow around it]. And if you fail to do so, when in contact with the world of conditions, karmic consciousness will be stirred up. Even if you do actually cut off and put a stop to all karmic consciousness, that is falling into the heretical path of dead emptiness. Then in the immaculate state that is produced, you convince yourself you've attained sainthood or enlightenment. Continue in this way and you will become arrogant; attached to this state, you will become as if demon-possessed. Entangled in the world, deluding others with your ignorance, you end up committing serious offenses, betray the trust others have in the Dharma, and obstruct the path of awakening.

Commentary

These are exhortations or admonishments – stern warnings – and Boshan reaches his stride toward the end of this third section. They must have been relevant for the people around him. I trust they are relevant for you too.

In the present context, discriminating consciousness and karmic consciousness (already mentioned in section one) are basically the same delusion. As long as the delusive nature of all such consciousness – and thus the great matter of life-and-death – is not decisively broken through, there is a great temptation to try and cut oneself off from it and deny it.

The point of this section is simple but profound: such suppression doesn't work. The very attempt is an activity of deluded consciousness. No attempt to resolve it within the framework of consciousness will work. On the other hand, in Great Doubt, all activities of consciousness naturally come to an end of their own accord. They are not suppressed.

About forty years ago my Dharma Granddad Zenkei Shibayama stated:

Often I come across people who just naively believe that samadhi in art, or no-mind in expert skill, is the same as that of Zen because of their superficial resemblance. According to them, there can naturally be dancing Zen, painting Zen, piano-playing Zen, or laboring Zen. This is an extremely careless misunderstanding. They have failed to see the basic difference between Zen and psychological absorption in an art or skill.

[ZCM, 75 rev.]

61

There certainly is genuine Zen action. From where does it arise? – That is the point. It is not merely a matter of mental state, psychological absorption, or suppression. A crucial concern for us as we work this out in work, and play, in the world. Alone with a crying baby – or a dying loved one – what do you do?

4. The Disease of Emptiness

If you're unable to arouse the Doubt when practicing Zen, you may come to regard the physical and mental worlds as utterly emptied, with nothing at all to cling to and nothing to hold onto. Unable to discern your own body and mind or the world around you, denying inner and outer, you make everything into one emptiness. Then you believe this emptying to be Zen, and the one who emptied it all to be a Buddha. You imagine that the four postures of going, staying, sitting, and reclining are done within emptiness. This too is simply your wavering mind; it is not Zen.

Continuing in this way, you end up in false emptiness, sunk in dark ignorance. Attached to it, you become as if demon-possessed and proclaim that you've attained enlightenment. All because you fail to realize that what you're doing has nothing to do with true Zen inquiry. If you genuinely inquire, with one koan you'd arouse this Doubt and wield it as a razor-sharp sword – whoever comes in contact with its blade will be annihilated. Otherwise, even though you may reach a state of emptiness where no thoughts arise, it is still ignorance and far from final.

Commentary

Don't get attached, even to "emptiness"! From the outside, it may sound like nonsense: If there's nothing, how can you be attached? And yet, that's exactly what can happen. Through proper practice and lifestyle, it is fairly easy to get free from most attachments. You can even get quite skillful at it. Then you abide for a while in your pretty little hole, stinking up the place.

This will not do. One real koan, properly applied, will do. Now, what will **you** do: Spend the rest of your life wavering between the plague of endless doubts and the futility of dead emptiness or once and for all break through your Great Doubt? Dahui, mentioned in the introductory lecture, stated: "this very lack of anywhere to get a grip is the time to let go of your body and your life" (*SF* 12 rev.).

Firm in Great Trust and motivated by Great Doubt, in sustained practice, let it all go. Don't even abide in any "emptiness" that remains. Boshan clears the way by sealing off every possible escape.

5. The Disease of Speculation

If you're unable to arouse the Doubt when practicing Zen, you may end up speculating with your karmic consciousness over the koans of old, sloppily scratching the surface. Then you declare it to be the whole truth, or at least half, as absolute, as relative, this as lord and that as vassal, unity attained [兼帶], clear and simple words, and so on, all the while praising yourself for your superior understanding. Even if you could interpret and explain away each and every one, spewing out the words of old as your own, this too is simply your wavering mind; it is not Zen.

You don't realize that you're merely taking the words and phrases of old and chewing them like balled-up cotton thread, unable to either swallow them or spit them out. How can such things create paths of liberation for others? How can they lead others to genuine insight? On the other hand, if you arouse this Doubt and throw yourself into it, then without waiting until the end of your life, karmic consciousness will cease of its own accord and entangling interpretations will naturally be put to rest.

Commentary

This fifth section on attachment to speculation is similar to the first one on intellectual attachment. "Chewing gum Zen": in mouth and mind it tastes good for a moment – maybe even blow a couple of bubbles with it – but soon it loses its taste. "Cotton candy Zen": it dissolves without satisfying our real hunger.

A number of Zen terms are mentioned here. These expressions were obviously bandied about – chewed on momentarily then summarily spat out – in Boshan's time. For example, "unity attained" is the fifth of the *Five Ranks* [五位] of Dong-shan Liangjie [Tozan Ryôkai 洞山良价 807-869]. A profound poetic expression of Zen by the co-founder of the Sôtô tradition. How tempting to speculate on and dumbly repeat such living expressions! And with it the life is gone. Boshan's attitude toward such speculation and Zen talk is crystal clear.

Tell me, how do you express it here and now? In the introductory lecture, I mentioned the koan about both speech and silence being relative; how then can we be free? Without resorting to Zen rhetoric, how do you express it? [*Silence*]

> *And when two lovers woo,*
> *They still say "I love you."*
> *On that you can rely.*
> ["As Time Goes By" lyrics by Herman
> Hupfeld featured in 1942 film *Casablanca*]

Once karmic consciousness comes to an end, do all our other entanglements also cease just like that? Let me make it relevant for present purposes: If awakening is total and immediate, why is practice endless? The sun rises at a certain moment, and with it day breaks and all is clearly illumined; the snow and ice, however, take time to break up and melt. A baby is born at a certain moment, though it may take years to walk, talk, and help others. (See *ZM* 153.)

Similarly, genuine awakening is by nature immediate, total, and complete; working it out in this world, in every aspect of our actions, speech, and thought is another matter. There is practice to arouse and break through the Great Doubt; there is also practice afterward. Don't neglect either one, or confuse one with the other.

Dahui was fond of stating: "Just get to the root, don't worry about the branches" (*SF* 2, 45, 109). In the present context: Get to the root now; in time the branches will flower. Practice must culminate in awakening – and be endless. How does practice culminate in awakening? And how is it endless? Mere speculation will not do. Wumen [Mumon 無門 1183-1260], in comments on the first case of his *Gateless Barrier*, stated: "With your whole body, arouse this one Doubt Block" [通身起箇疑團].

6. The Disease of Spirits

If you're unable to arouse the Doubt when practicing Zen, you may conclude: "Body and mind are dependent on the confluence of fleeting conditions. However, within all of this, there is one thing that comes and goes, free in both motion and rest, without form or substance. Shining from the sense organs. Spread out, it fills the universe; gathered in, not a dust mote remains!" With such an understanding, you fail to even try and arouse this Doubt or to truly inquire, presuming instead that you have completed the great matter. This too is simply your wavering mind; it is not Zen.

You fail to realize that what you are doing is not breaking through the *samsaric* mind of life-and-death [生死心] at all, but instead delighting in such understanding – self-deluded playing with spirits. When the last light of your eyes falls to the ground [death comes], you'll lose your precious hold. Then you'll be dragged about by your so-called spirits and have to repay your karmic debts. If you're able to accrue plenty of good karma, you may be reborn into the realm of humans or gods. Then facing death again, you'll find yourself crying: "The Buddha Dharma has no saving power!" Slandering the Buddha Dharma like this, you'll fall into the hell of hungry ghosts – and heaven knows how long you'll take to get out of that. You better find a true Dharma friend and inquire into this with them, for your complacent spirit will be of no help here.

Commentary

In this section on the disease of (believing in) spirits, Boshan plays on the believers' fears in order to rouse them to truly practice. Enamored with their speculations, the mental constructs are objectified, turned into something – what Boshan calls spirits. Then the believer is possessed, trapped by them in endless confusion.

What delusions remain for you? Give yourself fully and **see through now**. Then work even harder to disperse any entanglements that remain.

7. The Disease of Acting Out

If you're unable to arouse the Doubt when practicing Zen, you may think: "Eyes see, ears hear, the tongue speaks, the nose smells odors, hands grasp, feet run. All this is the true nature of the spiritual self!" You then conclude that you're enlightened and go about eyeballing people, bending an ear, pointing at this and kicking at that, thinking it's all the personification of Buddha Dharma. But this too is simply your wavering mind; it is not Zen.

Of old, such nonsense has been compared to temporary insanity, or likened to sitting in the master's formal chair with a frightening scowl frozen on your face. What good will all that do when you're facing death? Even worse are those who transmit this stuff to the next generation and accept offerings from the faithful without the least bit of shame. If someone asks about the Dharma, they yell or let out a big laugh. They have never truly inquired themselves, so they cannot cut through their *samsaric* life-root. In such a situation, even countless good deeds become the handiwork of the devil. And all because they fail to recognize that where they have reached is far from final.

Commentary

Here Boshan returns to the disease of imitating Zen actions. He lashes out at this corruption in later sections as well. Such "performance Zen" must have been rampant – unlike here and now! [*Laughter*]

In sections six and seven, Boshan mentioned:

Body and mind are dependent on the confluence of fleeting conditions. However, within all of this, there is one thing that comes and goes, free in both motion and rest, without form or substance. Shining from the sense organs. Spread out, it fills the universe; gathered in, not a dust mote remains!

Eyes see, ears hear, the tongue speaks, the nose smells odors, hands grasp, feet run. All this is the true nature of the spiritual self!

Such statements must have been popular at the time, and Boshan criticized them severely. However, they seem to have been cobbled together from statements found in classic Zen texts, such as *The Record of Linji* – the recorded sayings of the father of Rinzai Zen:

Followers of the Way, mind is without form and pervades the ten directions.
"In the eye it is called seeing, in the ear it is called hearing.
In the nose it smells odors, in the mouth it holds converse.
In the hands it grasps and seizes, in the feet it runs and carries."
Fundamentally it is one pure radiance; divided it becomes the six harmoniously united spheres of sense. If the mind is void, wherever you are, you are emancipated.

[*RL* 165 rev.]

67

Followers of the Way, if you wish to **be** Dharma, just have no doubts. "Spread out, it fills the entire Dharma realm; gathered in, the smallest hair cannot stand upon it." Distinctly and radiantly shining alone, it has never lacked anything.

[*RL* 287 rev.]

Where is the difference? Don't seek it in the words!

8. The Disease of Asceticism

If you're unable to arouse the Doubt when practicing Zen, you may become obsessed with a goal, preoccupied with achieving liberation, even undergo ascetic extremes. Not seeking warmth in winter or shade in summer. Asked for a piece of clothing, you give away your whole wardrobe. Content with freezing to death, you assume it to be liberation. Asked for food, you go without eating. Content with starving to death, you assume it to be liberation. It takes many forms but, generally speaking, comes from an intention to achieve and conquer. Thus, you end up deceiving the unwitting, who take you for a living Buddha or Bodhisattva and give all they can as offerings. People don't realize that this is abusing the Buddhist precepts and that all such acts are harmful.

Others, as Dharma practice, burn part of their bodies in sacrificial offerings, constantly worship the Buddha and confess their faults. From the worldly viewpoint, this is certainly virtuous. As far as true religious inquiry goes, however, it is quite meaningless. As has been said since of old: "Never get attached to Dharma-expressions." Worshipping the Buddha is one such Dharma expression, as is confession. All good things of the Buddha Dharma are so. I am not saying to dispense with them, but to do them with singleness of mind, thus to nourish the roots of all that is good. When your Dharma eye opens, you will see: sweeping away the burnt incense offerings is itself Buddha work.

Commentary

Especially during retreat, such practices may help purify and prepare. But they should not be mistaken for the Way. Even such noble acts can be corrupted by ego-self. Yes, sitting in meditation as well. Needless to say, it will not do to prematurely abandon such practices for "anything goes" self-indulgence either, as the last two sections below will show. "Obsessed with a goal [such as enlightenment], preoccupied with achieving liberation" is also not the Way – as Boshan states in the opening of this section.

This is true of the Great Doubt as well:

They [eyeless priests] tell practicers that unless they can raise the Great Doubt Block and then break through it, there can't be any progress in Zen. Instead of teaching them to live by the unborn Buddha-mind, they start by forcing them to raise this Doubt Block any way they can. People who don't have a doubt are now saddled with one. They've turned their Buddha-minds into Doubt Blocks. It's absolutely wrong.

[*UB* 57 rev.; 盤珪 35]

Bankei is absolutely right. This is not Great Doubt at all. It's Great Doubt gone awry – turned into a goal that self then tries to achieve. Great Doubt-Great Awakening is right under your own feet! Thus Boshan ends this section not with some superhuman, ascetic feat, but rather with the humble, everyday act of clearing away ash. See for yourself: with eye open, there's not a thing to achieve or to let go. Great Doubt, not to mention Great Awakening – as well as Bankei's "teaching them to live by the unborn Buddha-mind" – all are like last night's dream.

9. The Disease of Self-indulgence

If you're unable to arouse the Doubt when practicing Zen, you may fall into self-indulgent and wild ways. Meeting others, you sing, dance, and carry on. By the river and under trees you recite poetry, prattle, and laugh. Swaggering about busy places regardless of others, you convince yourself that you've resolved the great matter. When you see a worthy teacher open a meditation hall, establish rules for the sangha, do zazen, chant the name of the Buddha and do other virtuous acts, you let out a scornful laugh and curse him. Since you're not able to truly practice, you disturb others who are. Not knowing how to truly recite the sutras, worship, or confess your faults, you hinder others who do. Unable to truly inquire, you interrupt those who do. You can't open your own meditation hall, so you interfere with those who have. Unable to give a real Dharma talk, you interrupt those who do. Seeing a worthy teacher present a Dharma talk in front of a large congregation, you think up complicated questions and indulge in silly exchanges, giving a Zen shout or a slap. The worthy teacher recognizes such things as no more than ghostly spirits playing games. If he does not indulge you, however, you spread groundless rumors: "He doesn't understand the Dharma principle – what a pity!"

This is your wavering mind obsessed; if you continue this way, you will fall into demonic paths and commit serious offenses. Once your good karma is exhausted, you'll fall into the hell of incessant suffering. "Even good intentions have bad results." Alas!

Commentary

In this section, Boshan chillingly portrays those who try to deny their *dis-ease* by indulging in pathetic antics, parading around as accomplished men and women. Sobering words for all of us.

We are coming to the end of this retreat. Such sustained practice is precious indeed. But real practice is not something we sometimes **do** – for example, during intensive retreat or in daily practice. To be what it really is, it must come to be what we **are**. Then it is naturally forgotten.

10. The Disease of Putting on Airs

If you're unable to arouse the Doubt when practicing Zen, you may feel annoyed by the restrictions of the sangha. Some may want to go deep in the mountains where there's no one around. For a while they may be satisfied there, closing eyes and unifying mind with legs in full lotus and hands in grateful prayer. After a few months or years, however, they find themselves lost. Others, after sitting only a few days, turn to reading books and composing poetry. Self-indulgent, they shut the door and doze off. From a distance they seem dignified, but up close their decadence knows no bounds. Others are like juvenile delinquents greedily sneaking around, neither knowing shame nor fearing karmic retribution. Putting on airs and speaking as if they knew, they deceive the unwitting: "I met a great teacher! He transmitted the Dharma to me!" and so on. They herd the unwitting into their flock, then keep company with them or even make them their disciples. They act Zen-like and those under them follow suit. Unaware of their errors, they do not even know to reflect on themselves or feel regret, to seek out a worthy teacher or Dharma friend. Reckless and arrogant, they spread terrible lies. They are really pitiful. Recently, some have grown weary of the sangha and now seek out their own living quarters. It should send shivers up their spines!

If you are to genuinely seek the Way, I trust you'll drop such notions. Then you can inquire together with others in the sangha, and work together to keep an eye on things. Even if you cannot realize the Way, at least you will not fall into such corrupt paths. Practicing the Way, you must beware of these dangers.

Commentary

In this final section, Boshan continues with examples of "costume Zen," its excesses and shortcomings.

It can be a great temptation today as well to go off alone into nature and practice free of artificial restrictions. But unless your determination is solid and clear, you will likely go astray.

Three essentials are commonly mentioned for Zen practice: 1. Great Trust [大信根; literally "Great Root of Trust"], 2. Great Determination [大憤志], 3. Great Doubt. For this audience, I think a proper presentation of Great Trust and Great Doubt is enough. Great Determination can too easily turn into misguided and destructive willpower, as Boshan suggested in section eight on the disease of asceticism. Chinese Zen master Gaofeng Yuanmiao of the thirteenth century likened Great Determination to "the passion that possesses you when, on meeting the enemy who slew your father, you instantly want to cut him in two with your sword" (ZD 246).

The last paragraph underlines the value of practice together, supporting and being supported by each other. The final line warns us to beware of dangers. The term here translated as "beware" is the same Chinese character for the "Exhortations" in the title. Boshan ends by reminding us to exhort or admonish ourselves.

I trust that during this retreat you have come up against whatever keeps you from total immersion. Continue the work we have earnestly begun here: see into it, work through it, then let it go. Throw yourself into daily life as you have thrown yourself into practice here.

As mentioned in the introductory lecture, if your doubt is real, far from interfering with your daily life, it will be just what is needed. Embracing your own doubt, you can open up to others, make room for them, respond directly to their real needs. In this way, relations with others can be transformed. Here, the Zen Buddhist tradition – and me as one poor representative – still has much room to learn and grow. Thank you for your precious participation and for listening so intently.

NOTES

Revised version of lectures given in 2010 during retreats in the U.S., Japan, and throughout Europe.

The translations from Chinese, especially Boshan's *Exhortations*, would not have been possible without the great assistance of my colleague Kenji Kinugawa at Hanazono University. Colleagues and scholar-monks Zenkei Noguchi, Eirei Yoshida, and Takuma Senda at Hanazono University, Juhn Ahn of the University of Toronto, Julianna Lipschutz of the University of Pennsylvania's East Asian Collection, and Jerry H. Yu of the Max Planck Institute in Munich also offered valuable comment. Any mistakes are my own. I look forward to frank feedback from readers.

Boshan ["Mount Bo" 博山] is actually the name of the mountain where Boshan was active; like many masters, he came to be known as such. He is also known as Wuyi Yuanlai [無異元来] and Dayi [大艤]. He left home in his teens and took up Tiantai [天台] study and practice. Later his Zen master was Wuming Huijing [無明慧經1548-1618; see *ED* 95-6], a severe teacher who persistently rejected Boshan's initial insights and realizations. Boshan eventually broke through watching a man climb a tree. He then studied the precepts before finally teaching at Mount Bo. Several major Dharma heirs are listed for Boshan.

A lay disciple of Boshan wrote a preface dated 1611 for the larger work of which this *Exhortations* forms one part; Chinese, Korean, and Japanese editions have been published.

The Chinese text, along with Japanese *kokuyaku*[國譯] used for this translation:『國譯禪宗叢書』第参巻(東京: 國譯禪宗叢書刊行會, 1921). Compare 卍新纂續藏經 X63n1257_p0762c09(00) − X63n1257_p0764a14(03). Text critique and other materials in Japanese related to Boshan can be found in articles by Yûkei Hasebe [長谷部 幽蹊], Institute for Zen Studies, Aichi Gakuin University.

An English translation of short excerpts from Boshan's *Exhortations* was published back in 1959 in *The Practice of Zen* by Chang Chen-chi (see *PZ*) pp. 72-73. More recently, Sheng Yen's *Attaining the Way: A Guide to the Practice of Chan Buddhism* (Boston: Shambhala, 2006) includes excerpts translated by Guogu (Jimmy Yu), pp. 19-22.

Enjoying the Way

Enjoying the Way is the title of an early Chinese Zen poem that will be presented here for the first time in English translation. But let me begin with some introductory remarks.

Recently, I have been traveling in Europe and North America. Buddhist statues are everywhere: in shops, gardens, living rooms. What is their appeal, even for many who do not consider themselves Buddhist?

These statues, often of a Buddha seated in meditation, give a sense of composure or calm repose. The statues are of varying quality, but the better ones express imperturbable calm, a boundless composure that cannot be disturbed. This is a central facet of Buddhism.

But that is not all. There is also a boundless joy. For example, look at the garish "laughing Buddha" statues that greet you at the entrance to Chinese restaurants worldwide, or better yet, at the fine ink paintings depicting the legendary Hanshan [Kanzan 寒山 eccentric Chinese "Cold Mountain" monk].

Calmness and joy might even seem conflicting attitudes: if really calm, you're not joyful; if joyful, you're not calm. Yet these two — and much more — are clearly expressed in fine Buddhist sculpture, painting, and so on.

From where do this boundless calm and this boundless joy arise? These concrete depictions in wood or metal or on paper are actually abstract embodiments of awakening. What is that? It is what we are here to realize and go beyond.

Hanshan and Shide,
by Liang-kai (Chinese;
12th-13ᵗʰ century)

There is much confusion surrounding Zen Buddhist practice – and some of it is related to this imperturbable calm and boundless joy. For example, Zen practice is described as letting things calmly and naturally unfold. Others speak of it as a willful striving to break through to a joyous enlightenment. Like a poorly made Buddha image, such descriptions present merely one facet in a distorted manner.

Zen practice is not willful striving. You will never get there by mere will power. In fact, you do not need more energy than you now have. You **do** need to focus on the matter at hand, to properly direct that energy and not waste or disperse it. Throughout the retreat, we will learn how to do this.

Is Zen practice then a matter of letting things naturally unfold? Zen Buddhism **is** simple and natural. Buddhism, however, is not just a physical posture, nor is it merely a mental discipline. Since of old, Buddhism has been described as a practice of body, speech, and mind. Many people **speak** of Zen as simple and natural. But are **they** simple and natural? Ask one real question, or look at the lives they live.

What about us? Can we really let ourselves **be as we are**? Can we just let everything be as it is? More to the point, **should** we let everything – problems, pain, living and dying, good and evil – just be as it is? If we cannot discern this, of what use is our practice?

What motivates you in your practice and in your life? What fuels and drives you? Is your practice being fueled now? This intense retreat will likely be difficult, cause discomfort, even pain at times. Why are you doing it? Is it because you have realized the greater *dis-ease* of ignoring it?

It is like having a high fever. You go to the doctor and he examines you, perhaps prescribes medicine, suggests an injection, or even admits you to the hospital. Would you then say: "But the treatment must not cause any discomfort!" Stubborn illness may require bitter medicine. We certainly don't want to **cause** discomfort, but neither can we ignore the underlying *dis-ease* that we do have.

With proper treatment, the fever breaks and health returns. You know it, are glad and rejoice. That is what we are doing here. By proper practice, *dis-ease* naturally comes to an end. Is this worth looking into and even tolerating some discomfort? I leave it to you to decide.

....

I will also touch on relationships, love, and caring. Zen monastic life seems to downplay such "worldly" concerns. After all, monastics have left the world, have left home and family to devote themselves to the Way. Despite the significant role that lay Zen has played, monastics tend to assume that it is a minor exception to the monastic norm.

This must change; indeed, it already is changing. In 2007, head abbot Keidô Fukushima of the major Rinzai monastery complex of Tôfukuji in Kyoto stated: "While American Zen has certainly learned a great deal from Japanese Zen, I think it is now time for American Zen to stand on its own two feet. In contrast with the 'monastic Zen' of Japan, American Zen is essentially a 'lay Zen'" [*SLP* xvii]. And this phenomenon is not limited to America.

The joys and sorrows of family, home, and career are not the focus of monastic life – how could they be? But make no mistake: Zen Buddhism overflows with great compassion and with precious practical guidance for all. Monastic Zen may be limited to the monastery; Zen Buddhism is not.

What is needed here and now – in our home and work, among our family, friends, and co-workers? The answer is not found in an ancient Chinese text or behind monastery walls. It is our task to find out by opening up and seeing for ourselves. Then we can appreciate the greatness of the Zen Buddhist tradition and bring it to life in our world rather than make it an artificial accessory or ill-fitting appendage.

Presiding over rituals and memorial services, Japanese Zen priests and nuns played an important role in Japanese society. They have little place in ours. In fact, they are becoming irrelevant in Japan as well.

The Japanese priest is not a useful model for us. We do not live 300 years ago in Edo Japan – or 2,500 years ago at the foot of the Himalayas. All pomp and circumstance aside, what Japanese priests do in their **job** (and that's what it is) is no more "religious" or worthy, no more important or valuable, than what we do in ours. We are not second-class because we are lay people.

Monastic or lay, we devote our lives to practice. What is that? Is it what you're doing now? At any rate, it is not leaving one home for another, not renouncing one world to enter another, as made clear by Linji, the father of Rinzai Zen. [See *RL* 188.] It is certainly not a matter of replacing one set of clothes, hairdo, or given name with another.

....

One thing we can learn from monastic life is the value of **constant, sustained** practice, a **life** of practice. As valuable as retreat is, practice must continue throughout daily life. Monastics in that sense have it easy since lay people provide for them.

Lay people on the other hand practice in the midst of the world, contributing to society and supporting their families. In that sense, we must be at least as dedicated and committed as monastics. Retreats like this are proof that we can be; sustained practice at my hermitage in Kyoto provides an opportunity to take it further.

Devote yourself wholeheartedly to sustained practice for a week, a month, or years if you can. I myself did so; it was invaluable. It provides a good start, a solid foundation. But we cannot remain there; we must go beyond that, to truly **bring it home**.

Whether monastic or lay, Zen Buddhism is not an escape from *dis-ease*, nor is it a denial of our daily concerns. Put simply, Zen is about seeing into the source of those concerns so that they can be truly addressed. Zen practice offers ways to do this, including warnings about dangers on the way. The following is from the Ming dynasty Zen monk Boshan [Hakusan 博山 1575-1630]:

Practicing Zen, the worst thing is to become attached to quietness, because this will cause you to be engrossed in dead stillness without realizing it. People tend to dislike disturbances, but they don't mind quietness. Having lived amidst the noise and restlessness of worldly affairs, once you experience the joy of quietness, you crave it like the sweet taste of honey or a long slumber after hard work. It's difficult to recognize your mistake.

[*PZ* 67 rev.]

做工夫、最怕耽著靜境、使人困於枯寂、不覺不知。動境人厭、靜境多不生厭、良以行人一向處乎喧鬧之場、一與靜境相應、如食飴食蜜、如人倦久喜睡、安得自知耶。

X 63, 756a-b

Enough about monastics not knowing our problems! After all, monastics may not be familiar with changing diapers or paying taxes, but they were born into this world just like us. As a matter of fact, when it comes to dead stillness, **they** are the ones in greatest danger. We don't have the luxury to fall into it – at least for very long. Here and now, let us all together, monastic and lay, vow to give ourselves fully to practice and support each other as we do so.

....

Genuine Zen, including Zen texts, reveals both the **way** to get home and **where** that home really is. What is this way, this path? Are you on it now? Do you sense it? Where's the peace, the real home that you seek? And if you seek to leave home as a monastic, where is that home-leaving to be found?

When all the activities of consciousness have been stilled, as happens in real zazen, an entrance is found. True practice begins when, to paraphrase Linji, the activities of the ceaselessly seeking self are brought to rest. [See *RL* 155.] The activities of ego-self come to a full and complete stop.

Even in sound sleep, when self is temporarily disengaged, it has not come to a full and complete stop. For the self-complex returns the moment you wake from sleep. Every morning you **wake up as yourself**, and every night you let go of yourself as you fall asleep. While thoughts, emotions, and so on are somewhat subject to conscious control, the self-complex itself is beyond conscious control. You are subject to it; it is not subject to you.

Do you see how pervasive and total the *dis-ease* of self is? Do you see why Zen Buddhism is not concerned with states of consciousness or experiences, however subtle or enlightening? Such states and experiences are still states and experiences of the self.

And do you see why sitting through the nights in sustained zazen is a hallowed Zen Buddhist practice? Conscious delusions can be dealt with fairly easily – after all, they are conscious. So-called unconscious or non-conscious delusions cannot be dealt with so easily. It is not enough just to stabilize and quiet consciousness a while, for the self-complex remains. This is why many people attempt meditation for some time, then grow disillusioned with it and give up. Failing to penetrate the surface, they are honest enough to recognize that their minds are still going in the same old circles.

As you'll see, it's not difficult to sit through the night if you're practicing properly. And this helps to dislodge not only the conscious delusions but also the unconscious delusions. These unconscious delusions are what lie at the core of the self-delusion that is the delusion-of-self. Who wakes up every morning and falls asleep every night? If you really knew that, would you struggle in confusion during the day?

Unconscious delusions will not be uprooted easily. We have been grasping onto them and identifying with them all of our lives. They have become what we **are**. They're not going to disappear just because you hear a lecture about them or sit in meditation for a while.

With patient and proper practice, however, it's not difficult – for they **are** delusions, and they cannot persist if we do not feed them. A simple example: we may not even be conscious of some of our predilections and fixed views. But they can be strong and stubborn. So when we encounter someone, these preconceptions start to work and we end up encountering **them**, not the person in front of us. With patient and sustained practice, those preconceptions unravel and lose their hold. This allows us to see others for who they really are, rather than who we think they are. It allows us to see who and what we really are too.

....

When hungry, eat;
Tired, sleep.
Fools laugh at me,
But the wise know its wisdom.

When tired, sleep – and we were just discussing the virtue of sitting through the nights! (*Laughter*) This is one of the most famous quotes from *Enjoying the Way*.

Zen **is** eating when hungry, sleeping when tired. But isn't that what we all do anyway? Is it? How easily the deluded self trips over its own delusions. The early Chinese Zen master Huihai [Ekai 慧海] was asked by a *Vinaya*-precepts teacher about this:

"Reverend, do you still make efforts in your practice of the Way or not?"
Huihai: "Yes, I do."
"What efforts do you make?"
Huihai: "When hungry, eat; tired, sleep."
"Everybody does that. Aren't they making the same efforts as you?"
Huihai: "No they're not."
"Why not?"
Huihai: "When they eat they're not eating, but instead are preoccupied with a hundred different desires. When they sleep they're not sleeping, but instead are plagued by a thousand thoughts. So they're not the same."

81

The *Vinaya* teacher made no reply.

[*LA* 67 rev.]

有源律師來問。和尚修道還用功否。師曰。用功。曰如何用功。師曰。饑
來喫飯困來即眠。曰一切人總如是同師用功否。師曰。不同。曰何故不
同。師曰。他喫飯時不肯喫飯。百種須索。睡時不肯睡。千般計校。所以
不同也。律師杜口。

T 51, 247c

When hungry, eat. Simple enough? And yet, as a matter of fact, when we eat
we are often preoccupied with all kinds of things. Does anyone not recognize this?
Huihai was very kind in his answer.

Nowadays, many people in the First World have forgotten what hunger is
– we snack so compulsively that we don't have a chance to experience real hunger.
We eat when we're **not** hungry and that's a **huge** problem. We eat to relieve stress
and boredom. We even have a bizarre term for it: comfort food. Blindly seeking to
soothe our discomfort, we indulge in comfort food.

When hungry, eat. See how hard it is? – Because it's so simple! What gets in
the way? When you see that, the Buddhist path opens underfoot.

Linji spoke of putting to rest the activities of the seeking self. In other words,
the self that seeks for some enlightenment experience, seeks to escape from discomfort by eating or by fasting, seeks to be satisfied the way it is. **That** very self
comes to its own end. How to do this is the subject of our retreat.

And once the seeking self has come to rest, then we can start afresh, in the
midst of our busy lives, responding to the real needs of the world and of others.
Zen practice is not escaping from things. That is precisely what Zen practice is –
not escaping from anything. It is seeing what really is, being what you really are.

....

Let go in front, let go behind, let go in between:
Gone beyond all that is,
Mind released in every way,
You do not come again to birth and decay.
[*DHP* #348; *ZB* 22, 131 rev.]

This verse is from the *Dhammapada*, a well-known Buddhist text from the
Theravada canon. According to the commentaries, Gotama Buddha spoke these
words to an acrobat doing somersaults balanced atop a tall bamboo pole.

The acrobat, named Uggasena, was engaged in his craft. Like us, he was a
layperson working. Do you think his mind wandered when he worked? Does your
mind wander when you work? Does it wander when you do zazen? Do you think
your position is any safer or more secure than his? If you do, you're not doing zazen
– you're dreaming.

Upon hearing Gotama's verse, layman Uggasena, engaged in his work – balanced on top of a bamboo pole! – "attained arahantship." In other words, was liber-

ated. Do you think you're any different?

"Let go in front, let go behind ..." Commentaries explain that this refers to past and future. Nothing new here: we should not get hung up with the past or be preoccupied with the future. This much is common sense.

And yet, how often is your zazen lost in past memories or future plans? Indeed, it is necessary to be fully present in the present. Without this, we cannot even begin practice.

The real point, however, is what follows: "let go in between" – that is, let go in the middle, let go of the present as well. It is certainly important to let go of both past and future. But if you're trying to balance in "the present moment," you're still stuck. In 1775, Samuel Johnson said: "Patriotism is the last refuge of a scoundrel." In the present context, "Present moment is the last refuge of the self."

Where is this present moment – Now? Or is it now? How about now? Can you contain it? Does it contain you? Freed of past and future, **now** is the delusion ego-self maintains in order to preserve itself. Look! There is no present moment, nor is there any self in the present moment. As Gotama's verse makes clear, by letting go of the past, the future – and the present – one is "Gone beyond all that is, Mind released in every way, You do not come again to birth and decay." This is what Buddhism is all about. It is **not** being in the present. [See *BWS* 81, 196.] Now, where are you?

....

A kind of calm courage is necessary to see this practice through and let the seeking self come to rest once and for all. How do you practice with self to bring an end to self? If you are entangled in self-delusion, you need to practice in a way that lets it go. Otherwise, you may end up increasing the delusive seeking.

There are practices to help bring the self-delusion to rest. There are also practices for when the self-delusion has been laid to rest. Then the real work begins. For example, in complete openness, we can heal emotional damage and really help others and ourselves – and be helped by them.

One day years ago, after a hard day's work at university, I came home and got angry with my teenage son over something. He responded that I was blowing it out of proportion and that my anger wasn't just about him. Some parents might say that's exactly the kind of excuse teenagers will give. But he's no dummy. He was right. He had the calm courage to respond that way, and it made me realize that I had carried some emotional baggage home and dumped it on him. At that moment, he became my teacher.

Now I am there for my son when he tires of the race. And sometimes we enjoy running beside each other, sharing our experience.

In the throes of no-self awakening, nothing remains – all delusions are gone without a trace. And yet, some delusions will probably return – in a certain situation, you may find old patterns of emotion and thought arising, those old gears churning again. We need to be aware of this and see through them, thankful for being shown our blind spots and weaknesses. This kind of practice is at least as important as awakening.

Enjoying the Way

[*Ledao ge/Rakudô-ka* 樂道歌]

attributed to **Nanyue Mingzan**

[*Nangaku Myôsan* 南嶽明瓚 *a.k.a. Lanzan "Lazy Zan"* 懶瓚; *eighth century.*]

I

1. Serenely carefree, nothing to change;	兀然無事無改換
2. Carefree, what need for words?	無事何須論一段
3. Real mind doesn't scatter,	眞心無散亂
4. So no need to stop worldly cares.	他事不須斷
5. The past is already past,	過去已過去
6. The future can't be reckoned.	未來更莫算
7. Sitting serenely carefree,	兀然無事坐
8. Why would anyone pay a call?	何曾有人喚
9. Seeking to work on things outside –	向外覓功夫
10. It's all foolishness!	總是癡頑漢

II

11. As for provisions, not one grain;	糧不畜一粒
12. If a meal is offered, just gobble it up.	逢飯但知喫
13. Worldly folk full of needless care,	世間多事人
14. Always chasing, they never get it.	相趁渾不及

III

15. I neither desire heavenly realms,	我不樂生天
16. Nor want blessings in this world.	亦不愛福田
17. When hungry, eat;	饑來即喫飯
18. Tired, sleep.	睡來即臥眠
19. Fools laugh at me,	愚人笑我
20. But the wise know its wisdom.	智乃知賢
21. It's not being stupid –	不是癡鈍
22. It's what we originally are.	本體如然

IV

23. When you have to go, go;	要去即去
24. When you have to stay, stay.	要住即住
25. Over shoulders, a ragged robe;	身被一破納
26. Below, bare feet.	脚着孃生袴
27. Talking, talking, more and more –	多言復多語
28. Always leads to mistakes.	由來反相誤
29. If you want to save others,	若欲度衆生
30. Better work on saving yourself!	無過且自度

V

31. Don't rashly seek the true Buddha;
32. True Buddha can't be found.
33. Does marvelous nature and spirit
34. Need tempering or refinement?
35. Mind is this mind carefree;
36. This face, the face at birth.
37. Even if the kalpa-rock is moved,
38. It alone remains unchanged.

莫謾求真佛
真佛不可見
妙性及靈臺
何曾受勳鍊
心是無事心
面是孃生面
劫石可移動
箇中難改變

VI

39. Carefree is just that –
40. What need to read the words?
41. With the root of delusive self gone,
42. All falls into place right where it is.

無事本無事
何須讀文字
削除人我本
冥合箇中意

VII

43. Rather than get worn out over this and that,
44. In the woods, serene, just take a nap.
45. Raise your head and the sun's already high;
46. Scrounge for food, then wolf it down.

種種勞筋骨
不如林間睡兀兀
舉頭見日高
乞飯從頭喰

VIII

47. Intent on getting good results,
48. You merely fall deeper into ignorance.
49. Try to grasp, it can't be gotten;
50. Let go and there it is.

將功用功
展轉冥朦
取則不得
不取自通

IX

51. I have one "word";
52. With it, all concepts and relations gone.
53. Clever explanations cannot get at this,
54. Only mind conveys it.

吾有一言
絕慮忘緣
巧說不得
只用心傳

X

55. Again this single "word,"
56. Directly expressed without medium.
57. Smaller than small,
58. Originally without direction or place.
59. Originally whole and complete –
60. Not something strung together with effort.

更有一語
無過直與
細如毫末
本無方所
本自圓成
不勞機杼

86

XI

61. Lost in worldly cares   世事悠悠
62. Is far from mountain stillness.   不如山丘
63. Where pines obscure sunlight,   青松弊日
64. **Clear green streams flow on and on.**   碧澗長流
65. Lying down beneath wisteria vines,   臥藤蘿下
66. Head pillowed on smooth stone.   塊石枕頭
67. With mountain clouds as curtain   山雲當幕
68. And night moon as a hook.   夜月為鉤
69. Not rising for the emperor,   不朝天子
70. Why envy royalty?   豈羨王侯
71. Not even birth-death concerns me –   生死無慮
72. What remains to grieve over?   更須何憂

XII

73. Moon reflected in water has no fixed form;   水月無形
74. That's the way I always am.   我常只寧
75. Each and every thing as it is,   万法皆爾
76. Originally unborn.   本自無生
77. Sitting serenely carefree: 兀然無事坐
78. Spring comes, the grass grows green of itself.   春來草自青

Retreat Lectures

This song, a kind of free-style tone poem, is attributed to an early Chinese hermit-monk who lived in the eighth century. He is known as Nanyue Mingzan, but he was also called Lanzan, or "Lazy Zan." Little is known about him or his song. This is partly due to his affiliation with what came to be called the Northern School of Chinese Zen, in contrast to the Southern School of the Sixth Patriarch. No need to go into detail, but for sectarian and political reasons, this Northern School was eventually condemned for holding onto dualistic, gradual, step-by-step, "polishing-the-mirror" practices. Before long, this school disappeared. If you look at the poem, however, no such teachings or practices are mentioned.

In contrast to this Northern School, the Southern School of the Sixth Patriarch was lauded for its teaching of "originally there is not a thing" [本来無一物] and "immediate awakening" [頓悟] (often distorted in English as "sudden enlightenment" – a poor translation since it is neither sudden nor enlightenment. Sudden suggests quickness in time, whereas it is *im-mediate, un-mediated*. The self-confinements of time and space – not to mention the present moment – are gone. The self-separation that maintains such delusions has come to an end.)

About a century later, Linji (Rinzai in Japanese) took up this torch of immediate awakening. He even stated that the Buddhist teachings are toilet paper to wipe your butt with. [See *RL* 222-3.] But what are the teachings that **he** quoted and relied on? Lines found in *Enjoying the Way* were some of his favorites, as we will see.

The title 樂道歌 could be translated literally as "Song of Enjoying the Way," although it was probably not given that title or its present form until long after. At any rate, the title is not unique; it is generic and used for a whole genre of songs.

....

Who is Lazy Zan? In case 34 of *The Blue Cliff Record*, the following story is found. Lazy Zan secluded himself in a stone cave. The emperor heard of him and sent a messenger to summon him to court – the honor of a lifetime. The messenger announced the imperial command to the hermit-monk: "Reverend, you should rise and acknowledge the Imperial Benevolence!" Lazy Zan did not even answer but simply remained hunched over his cow-dung fire; he pulled out a roasted yam and began eating it. It was wintertime and snot ran down his chin. Finally, the messenger laughed and said: "Reverend, at least you could wipe the snot away!" "Why should I bother for a worldly man?" replied Lazy Zan. After all, he did not rise. The messenger returned and reported this to the throne. The emperor was filled with admiration. [*RL* 172 rev.; *T* 48, 173b] Hard to believe there is not **some** historical truth in such detail.

The Blue Cliff Record concludes the section on him with this eulogy: "Someone so pure and calm, so clear and direct as this, is not at the disposal of others; he just holds still, as though made of cast iron." [*BCR* 214] "Not at the disposal of others" – who is other to such a one?

....

89

What does this eighth-century ode to leisurely contentment have to do with us? If it merely celebrates the joys of a rustic life away from worldly concerns, well then it certainly has little to do with our lives, except perhaps as a dreamy ideal, like a Chinese landscape painting hung on our office wall. Something to remind us of how far away we are, perhaps allow a moment's escape into its jagged, misty contours.

But what if this song is singing about our reality – including our workaday world and family life? What does this ancient ode really have to say to us – nothing? Or perhaps everything?

....

Let us now return to the song, verse by verse. (The division into twelve verses is based on the rhyming tone scheme, which I have not attempted to imitate here. No such divisions exist in the four versions found in the Buddhist canon.)

I

1. Serenely carefree, nothing to change;	兀然無事無改換
2. Carefree, what need for words?	無事何須論一段
3. Real mind doesn't scatter,	眞心無散亂
4. So no need to stop worldly cares.	他事不須斷
5. The past is already past,	過去已過去
6. The future can't be reckoned.	未來更莫算
7. Sitting serenely carefree,	兀然無事坐
8. Why would anyone pay a call?	何曾有人喚
9. Seeking to work on things outside –	向外覓功夫
10. It's all foolishness!	總是癡頑漢

To give an impression of how subtle and nuanced this is, let me briefly unpack just the first four Chinese characters of the first line. The first two characters, pronounced in Japanese *gotsu-nen*, form a phrase I have translated as "serenely." The English expression "dead to the world" or "oblivious" could also be used. It is an ancient expression that brings to mind the Daoist image of a withered tree or dead ashes. Yet it can include a positive sense of towering and steadfast, ingenuous, uncontrived, unruffled, unhindered by affectation or conscious manipulation, ungraspable, beyond sensuous experience and knowing.

The third and fourth Chinese characters of this first line, pronounced in Japanese *bu-ji*, are translated here as "carefree." Literally, the two characters mean "no thing" (that is, no matter or no affair, nothing at all to do or accomplish). Like the previous phrase *gotsu-nen*, it includes a positive sense of free of all doings, free of things, done seeking, as-it-is with nothing superfluous. "Without a thing" is fairly literal, but "**contented** without a thing" captures it better. This was a favorite term of Linji and it expresses the essence of his Zen.

Sound foreign and opaque? Consider Meister Eckhart's Godhead as the "silent desert where distinction never gazed, where there is neither father nor son nor holy spirit" [*ML* 162] or his descriptions of the soul as eternally virgin and without hin-

90

drance, "as free as it was when it was not." [See *UW* 52-7, *WJ* 9ff, *MT* 140.] Now let us look at the first verse.

The first line sums up the entire song – it's all there. Realizing for ourselves what lies behind those first four Chinese characters, we should see that "nothing to change" (which completes this first line) is not merely passive acceptance but a matter of "doing nothing – **yet nothing is left undone.**" [See the Daoist classics *Dao De Jing* chapter 48 and *Zhuangzi* chapter 22.]

The second line playfully gives us words as it takes them away – for words are useful, but not necessary here. Zazen manuals give step-by-step instructions, and they are certainly useful. None is offered here – instead, the third and fourth lines directly and immediately point out the heart of the matter. No gradual practices in this poem; no means or methods for the ego-self to corrupt.

The sentiment of the fifth and sixth lines we've seen before; the seventh, which **repeats the first four characters of the first line,** speaks of sitting (meditation). What is this sitting that is serenely carefree? Is it sitting seeking to get there, or sitting that has arrived? Or is it sitting free of all such distinctions?

The eighth line is perhaps sung with self-effacing humor; why would anyone want to visit this old fart? We will return to this in verse eleven. The ninth and tenth lines are quoted by Linji in one of his most powerful statements:

A man of old said: "Seeking to work on things outside – It's all foolishness!" Just **be** every situation that arises, and wherever you stand is true. Whatever circumstances come, they cannot upset you. Even though you **bear the influence of past delusions or the karma from the five cardinal** sins, these of themselves become the ocean of emancipation!

[*RL* 186 rev.]

古人云。向外作[覓]工夫。總是癡頑漢。爾且隨處作主。立處皆真。境來回
換不得。縱有從來習氣五無間業。自為解脫大海。

T 47, 498a

This statement from *The Record of Linji* was used for many years at Kyoto Station as an advertisement for the Zen-affiliated university where I teach. Marvelous statement – although it may have been a bit over the top for many as they scurried by! What do you think they got from it? What do you get from it?

By the way, one edition of *Enjoying the Way* in the Buddhist canon has an apparent scribal error (內 instead of 向) so that line 9, "Seeking to work on things outside," reads "Seeking to work on things inside or outside." Suggestive, especially in light of Linji's take on it.

II

11. As for provisions, not one grain;	糧不畜一粒
12. If a meal is offered, just gobble it up.	逢飯但知喫
13. Worldly folk full of needless care,	世間多事人
14. Always chasing, they never get it.	相趁渾不及

A monk naturally has few provisions. But "not one grain" – what is he referring to? Line twelve speaks of gobbling up a food offering. Is this eating due to stress or boredom? Worrying and needlessly seeking, sitting endless hours in zazen: when will you **get it**?

You may feel frustrated at this point in your practice: working hard yet getting nowhere. It seems endless. But the content of consciousness **is** limited. Like the small, hourglass-shaped egg timer in the kitchen: turn it over and in a few minutes you can see that the top half is empty. Not one grain.

The practice we are doing will not be completed in a few minutes. If it's done properly, however, we can confirm for ourselves soon enough that the content of consciousness is limited.

Why doesn't it seem that way? Because although the restlessly seeking self turns over the timer, in a minute self grows anxious, bored, or confused – then turns it over again! And again. Well, in that case, it **is** endless. You will never get to the end – even though it is limited and only takes a few minutes.

That's what the seeking self, the wavering mind, does. Even when it attempts to practice or to meditate. A retreat is turning the timer over and seeing what happens if you leave it be and just sit through. Then you can confirm yourself that the content of consciousness is limited. No need to trust my words.

III

15. I neither desire heavenly realms,	我不樂生天
16. Nor want blessings in this world.	亦不愛福田
17. When hungry, eat;	饑來即喫飯
18. Tired, sleep.	睡來即臥眠
19. Fools laugh at me,	愚人笑我
20. But the wise know its wisdom.	智乃知賢
21. It's not being stupid –	不是癡鈍
22. It's what we originally are.	本體如然

Once the seeking self has come to rest of its own accord, the first two lines almost sing themselves. The next two lines could hardly be more prosaic: eating when hungry, lying down and closing one's eyes when drowsy. As already mentioned, these simple, daily acts are almost impossible for self to do purely and wholly – why is that? What gets in the way?

When hungry, eat – this isn't just about you. How many people in the world today don't **have** food to eat? See the challenge laid at our feet with these three words? To be "serenely carefree" is to hunger as long as one person cannot eat.

For the ceaselessly seeking self, nothing it comes across will give lasting satisfaction. Once the seeking self has come to rest, the most ordinary and commonplace is quite enough. "When hungry, eat; Tired, sleep." The fool indeed may laugh: You call that the summit of a life of religious practice? Yet how extraordinarily ordinary are the everyday, immediate events of our lives – when freed of tedious manipulations and self-centered seeking. Nothing esoteric, up in the clouds. Far from being dull or stupid, this is intrinsic wisdom. And it naturally works in the world.

The following statement of Linji overflows with the spirit of *Enjoying the Way* and ends paraphrasing lines seventeen to twenty:

As to Buddha Dharma, no effort is necessary. Just be ordinary and carefree: shitting, pissing, dressing, eating, and lying down when tired.
Fools laugh at me, but the wise understand.

[RL 185 rev.; cf. 282]

佛法無用功處。祇是平常無事。屙屎送尿著衣喫飯。困來即臥。愚人笑我。智乃知焉。

T 47, 498a

IV

23. When you have to go, go;	要去即去
24. When you have to stay, stay.	要住即住
25. Over shoulders, a ragged robe;	身被一破納
26. Below, bare feet.	脚着孃生袴
27. Talking, talking, more and more –	多言復多語
28. Always leads to mistakes.	由来反相誤
29. If you want to save others,	若欲度衆生
30. Better work on saving yourself!	無過且自度

The first two lines remind us that this is not merely indulging in quietism but rather doing what must be done. How much of our time is spent daydreaming, seeking to be somewhere else? The ragged robe and bare feet suggest freedom from attachment and from ambition, nothing superfluous, nothing remaining. Bare feet are literally "the leggings received from mother [at birth]" – spiritually naked and free.

Lines twenty-seven and twenty-eight return to the limit, the trap, of language, how words can get in the way. The last two lines require that we really see through the words. The first of our *Four Great Vows*: "Numberless beings – set free" [literally: "Vowing to set free numberless beings" 衆生無邊誓願度]. This is where, and how, we **begin** practice. Can you discern, in the last two lines, a precious warning about the ambitious desire to save others?

The tone and tenor of this verse, especially the first two lines, are again echoed in *The Record of Linji* – which seamlessly leads to the next verse:

Conforming with circumstances as they are, [the true follower of the Way] exhausts his past karma; accepting things as they are, he puts on his clothes. When he has to walk he walks, when he has to sit he sits. He doesn't have one thought of seeking Buddhahood.

[RL 171 rev.]

但能隨緣消舊業。任運著衣裳。要行即行。要坐即坐。無一念心希求佛果。

T 47, 497c

V

31. Don't rashly seek the true Buddha;	莫謾求眞佛
32. True Buddha can't be found.	眞佛不可見
33. Does marvelous nature and spirit	妙性及靈臺
34. **Need tempering or refinement?**	何曾受勳鍊
35. Mind is this mind carefree;	心是無事心
36. This face, the face at birth.	面是孃生面
37. Even if the kalpa-rock is moved,	劫石可移動
38. It alone remains unchanged.	箇中難改變

Why can't true Buddha be seen, without or within? Only the living and naked reality will do here, not statues or mind-states. As Linji was fond of saying: "True Buddha is without form." [See *RL* 228, 262, 263.]

There is much need for patient tempering and careful refinement. *Enjoying the Way* sings of the fundamental reality that is beyond all such tweaking and tampering. ("Nature" here refers to our original and true nature, not the world of nature.)

And where we end up is "this mind carefree." **You** – free of self. Done with seeking. Nothing transcendent or esoteric. Your face at birth. Or, if you seek to be more Zenistic, your original face before the birth of your parents.

The kalpa-rock moved or worn away refers to an endlessly long time. Even longer than some of those painful zazen periods. It – what is that? – remains unchanged. **This** – does it come or go, can it be tempered, tweaked, or tampered with? Relieve stress as much and as often as you like; you will never attain **this**.

VI

39. Carefree is just that –	無事本無事
40. What need to read the words?	何須讀文字
41. With the root of delusive self gone,	削除人我本
42. All falls into place right where it is.	冥合箇中意

The first two lines return to the theme of words and their limits. When you know, you know. Is there value then in reading these verses? Listen: Lazy Zan is laughing joyfully with us!

The term rendered as "the root of delusive self" also suggests striving for advantage over others. Once this is removed, we find that, at bottom, nothing was lacking in the first place. Then we cannot but endlessly work, with body, speech, and mind, with blood, sweat, and tears, for those who hunger and thirst. **That** is carefree (*bu-ji*) activity.

VII

43. Rather than wear yourself out over this and that,	種種勞筋骨
44. In the woods, serene, just take a nap.	不如林間睡兀兀
45. Raise your head and the sun's already high;	舉頭見日高
46. Scrounge for food, then wolf it down.	乞飯從頭喰

Is the author falling into dead passivity and quietism here? (How about you?) Or is there an unself-conscious dynamism at work, untouched by worldly ambition or desire?

"A day without work is a day without eating." Baizhang [Hyakujô 百丈 720-814], who made this his life's motto, is also credited with creating unique rules for the Zen monastery. He, along with Bodhidharma and Linji, is considered one of the founders of the Zen school.

It is said that when master Baizhang got old, his monks hid his tools to save him from the chore of working. When Baizhang could not find his tools that day, he did not work. But he also refused to pick up his chopsticks and eat. That was how seriously he lived by his own words: "A day without work is a day without eating." This was his Zen-at-work – brimming with wisdom and compassion.

Is this the same as "When hungry, eat"? Gobbling it up and wolfing it down? How would coal miners, trapped for weeks with little food, survive? If you just blindly accept these Zenistic expressions rather than breathe life into them, you and the expressions are both dead!

VIII

47. Intent on getting good results,	將功用功
48. You merely fall deeper into ignorance.	展轉冥朦
49. Try to grasp, it can't be gotten;	取則不得
50. Let go and there it is.	不取自通

Did you hear the flock of geese fly overhead in the early morning zazen?

Wild geese do not intend to leave traces, 鴈無遺蹤之意。
The water has no mind to absorb their image. 水無沈影之心。
ZS 461

You – you are the water, with no mind to receive the image. **You** – you are the geese flapping through boundless sky. Is this dead quietism, or the source of dynamic activity? It's all here, alive and well, every flapping wing flawlessly reflected – yet without self-conscious intent.

As if commenting on this, Rainer Maria Rilke wrote in the first of his *Duino Elegies*:

You *still* don't get it? Cast the emptiness out of your arms
into the space we breathe, so that the birds
may feel the expanding air with their deeper flight.
[Jeannette Stowasser translation]
*Weißt du's **noch** nicht? Wirf aus den Armen die Leere*
zu den Räumen hinzu, die wir atmen; vielleicht daß die Vögel
die erweiterte Luft fühlen mit innigerm Flug.

IX

51. I have one "word";	吾有一言
52. With it, all concepts and relations gone.	絕慮忘緣
53. Clever explanations cannot get at this,	巧說不得
54. Only mind conveys it.	只用心傳

After repeating that there is no need for words or language, he now raises his one word. If all concepts and relations are gone with it, what kind of word is that? The term for "convey" in the last line can also be translated as "transmit," suggesting the Zen Buddhist transmission of mind – by, for, to, as – mind. Mind transmitting mind. What kind of mind is this? Enough said.

X

55. Again this single "word,"	更有一語
56. Directly expressed without medium.	無過直與
57. Smaller than small,	細如毫末
58. Originally without direction or place.	本無方所
59. Originally whole and complete –	本自圓成
60. Not something strung together with effort.	不勞機杼

Again he raises this word – yet it's direct and unmediated. Is it his? Yours? Are you going to perfect or polish it? Realizing **this** – "Originally whole and complete" – we work with blood, sweat, and tears to perfect what should be perfected, to polish what needs to shine.

It is not a state of mind, not an experience or event, however lofty or illuminating. The self is certainly subject to such states and experiences. But that is not Zen. Thus, Linji speaks of the seeking self itself coming to an end. If the self-complex remains, any mind-state or experience, however profound or lofty, can become an entanglement, can do more harm than good. Beware!

XI

61. Lost in worldly cares	世事悠悠
62. Is far from mountain stillness.	不如山丘
63. Where pines obscure sunlight,	青松弊日
64. **Clear green streams flow on and on.**	碧澗長流
65. Lying down beneath wisteria vines,	臥藤蘿下
66. Head pillowed on smooth stone.	塊石枕頭
67. With mountain clouds as curtain	山雲當幕
68. And night moon as a hook.	夜月為鉤
69. Not rising for the emperor,	不朝天子
70. Why envy royalty?	豈羨王侯
71. Not even birth-death concerns me –	生死無慮
72. What remains to grieve over?	更須何憂

This verse, with stunning natural imagery, is the climax of the song. Don't take the images **too** literally. We don't have to be surrounded by mountain stillness or underneath wisteria vines – just not wrapped up in our selves.

Lines sixty-nine and seventy refer to the emperor's messenger. (See verse one, line eight, and p. 89 above).

XII

73. Moon reflected in water has no fixed form;	水月無形
74. That's the way I always am.	我常只寧
75. Each and every thing as it is,	万法皆爾
76. Originally unborn.	本自無生
77. Sitting serenely carefree:	兀然無事坐
78. Spring comes, the grass grows green of itself.	春來草自青

Line seventy-seven is identical with the seventh line of verse one. The last two lines are often quoted. Like much of the poem, these last two lines can be taken as mere passive resignation. To put it bluntly in my own poor language, "Sitting serenely carefree" is sitting without self. When you are truly without self, it is apparent that **all** is without self. Realizing this, the precious dignity of each and every thing is manifest. It is not passive resignation.

....

Let me briefly introduce a verse in praise of Lazy Zan from the Song dynasty master Xutang Zhiyu [Kidô Chigu 虛堂智愚 1185-1269]. With penetrating insight and superb literary skill, he is a Zen master's Zen master. The compact verse, four lines of four characters each, concisely sums up Lazy Zan's Zen – and much more:

Stone bed freezing cold.	石床冰冷。
Smell of dung-roasted yams.	糞火芋香。
Probe deep, here it is:	深撥淺得。
Flavor lingers everywhere.	滋味最長。

T 47, 1031a; 虛堂 159

The first two lines set the stage by giving much of what little is known about the man: Lazy Zan lived in a stone cave and happened to be roasting yams in a dung-fire when the imperial messenger arrived. Have you picked up the scent?

The third line has been freely rendered. Literally, the four characters say something like: "probe deep, attain shallow." This contains many allusions; it suggests that by deep and patient probing, what had seemed hard to reach finally appears close at hand. This refers to the roasted yams as well as to the result of thoroughgoing practice in service to all. Then the flavor lingers on, instead of becoming the stink of Zen.

Family, friends, and coworkers have made sacrifices so that you could be here for this retreat. Do make good use of the remaining time here and be grateful when you return home. Don't go back half-baked.

Just as you threw yourself into practice here, when you return to home and work, throw yourself into what needs to be done there. Then there will be no gap in your practice.

There **will** be challenges and problems for sure. Be grateful for them. Bow in thanks and they become your teacher. Then nothing can really get in the way; the fine flavor will linger everywhere.

....

Let me send you off with an excerpt from one more song delighting in the way:

> *Afoot and light-hearted I take to the open road,*
> *Healthy, free, the world before me,*
> *The long brown path before me leading wherever I choose.*
>
> *Henceforth I ask not good-fortune, I myself am good-fortune,*
> *Henceforth I whimper no more, postpone no more, need nothing,*
> *Done with indoor complaints, libraries, querulous criticisms,*
> *Strong and content I travel the open road.*
>
> *The earth, that is sufficient,*
> *I do not want the constellations any nearer,*
> *I know they are very well where they are,*
> *I know they suffice for those who belong to them.*
>
> *(Still here I carry my old delicious burdens,*
> *I carry them, men and women, I carry them with me wherever I go,*
> *I swear it is impossible for me to get rid of them,*
> *I am fill'd with them, and I will fill them in return.)*

Which great Zen master penned these lines? This is the opening of Walt Whitman's 1881 version of *Song of the Open Road*. "Need nothing" in the second verse could be a translation of *bu-ji*.

The last verse quoted is especially pertinent since it takes up the Bodhisattva ideal in a way that *Enjoying the Way* does not. What are these "delicious burdens"? Why can't they be gotten rid of? I leave them with you.

NOTES

Revised transcript of retreat lectures given throughout Europe and the States in the summer of 2010.

Translation based on『祖堂集』edition as found in「懶瓚和尚『樂道歌』攷–祖堂集研究會報告之三–」(土屋昌明, 衣川賢次, 小川隆)『東洋文化研究所紀要』第141冊, 125～195頁(2001.3).
Compare: *T* 49: #2036, 606b-c; 佛祖歷代通載卷第十四;
T 51: #2076, 461b-c; 景德傳燈錄卷第三十;
X 66, #1298, 744b-c; 禪門諸祖師偈頌下之上;
X 83, #1578, 424a-b; 指月錄卷之二.

The Record of Linji, Ruth Fuller Sasaki translator (Honolulu: University of Hawaii Press, 2009) was helpful detailing Linji's debt to *Enjoying the Way*.

The Japanese Rinzai commentary for Xutang's verse sums up the sectarian attitude toward Lazy Zan: "We don't admire this elder [that is, Lazy Zan]'s lineage style, but we do admire the purity of his practice." 虛堂下では此の老の家風を貴びはせぬ, 只だ工夫の純一を貴ふ.[虛堂 159]

APPENDIX

The Constant Practice of Right Effort

*(Revised version of the opening lecture for a
Zen Buddhist retreat at Pendle Hill in September 2008.)*

Thank you to everyone for your presence here. Simply and in a word, we have gathered for this retreat to put an end to, to come to the end of, "*dis-ease*" or *dukkha*. (*Dukkha* is a Buddhist technical term; it is also the first noble truth of Buddhism.) To put it another way, we are here to find true ease, to come to true rest, genuine health and wholeness – *real* stability.

Can we, by exerting effort, come to rest? Can we? You see how important it is to practice correctly. Or we end up chasing our own tail in an endless, fruitless effort.

The fourth noble truth is called the eightfold path, one of which is right effort – correct or proper effort. Clarifying and putting into practice this right effort is crucial. Otherwise, wrong effort only prolongs the *dis-ease* you are trying to cure; a fatal error.

This is the beginning of a retreat. As many of you have mentioned in your introductions, it is a precious opportunity for us to practice together, to support and be supported by each other in our practice. Right here and now, let us begin with right effort.

Do you see how striving to attain something, within or without, is itself prolonging the *dis-ease*? You may do it quickly or slowly, poorly or well, but after all it is a fruitless and futile effort, like chasing your own tail. It is not the right effort of Buddhism. To put it bluntly, trying to get somewhere other than where you are, trying to realize something or attain some state of mind, is part and parcel of the *dis-ease* that self is.

As you come to clearly see this through your own experience, to taste it, you can let go of wrong effort once and for all. Then your practice can naturally develop right effort untainted by self. Not that you cease to do anything! But you cease the frustrating and pointless practice of wrong effort, you stop chasing your own tail. Such wrong effort is a tremendous waste of energy. And it does not bring about true ease. In fact, it tends to create other problems instead.

Striving to get somewhere, to attain something, is wrong effort. Is it any better, however, to try and persuade myself that I'm okay as I am, that I don't need to do anything – after all, all beings have the Buddha nature, right? I trust you can already see what a deceptive and fruitless dead end this is. To put it bluntly, the self that is not at ease is trying to convince itself that it is. It doesn't work. Far from resolving anything, it tends to become an escape from actual problems. Clearly not right effort.

On the one hand striving to attain something, and on the other hand trying to convince myself that I'm okay when I'm not – both are symptoms of the same *dis-ease*. The self, through its own will power, striving to attain some enlightened state is like being dehydrated – and then deciding to run around the block a few times.

That will only make it worse. Trying to convince yourself that you're okay when you're not is like overeating to the point of nausea – and then deciding to wash it down with a banana split. Both are wrong effort. Seeing this much, let them both go, now and for good. Not because I say so, but because you see it through your own practice and experience.

This retreat is a precious opportunity to *see through* the delusive *dis-ease* that self is. Not mere ideas or notions *about* it. But to actually see through it, thus to let it go for good. One way to work on this is through the constant practice of right effort. The retreat and the meals as well are in silence. During the sittings we are not only silent but still. Not because we are prohibited from talking or moving, but because such noble silence and noble stillness are themselves right effort. We eloquently support each other in our practice without unnecessary talking or movement. These are themselves precious facets in our constant practice of right effort, whether eating, sitting, walking or going to the toilet.

If you are in good health, sitting through the nights together is also a natural part of this. Why? Do it and you will see how sitting through the nights is an integral part of the constant practice of right effort. However, if your health does not allow it, no problem; sitting through the nights does not equal right effort. If you sit through the nights as a huge, willful striving, that is wrong effort. Better to rest in your room, lying on your back and gently maintaining your focus below your belly so that when you wake up it is there before a thought arises. That is right effort.

In a sense, it has nothing to do with sleeping or staying up all night. This retreat is, however, a precious opportunity for sustained practice together. We have all made preparations, some of you have come a great distance, and our families and coworkers have made sacrifices so that we could be here. It is only natural to make best use of this opportunity and sit through the nights. No one will tell you what you must do, however. Finally you must decide for yourself.

This means not letting your momentary inclinations and passing fancies dictate what to do either. If your sitting is not yet firmly established in right effort, you may find yourself lost in thoughts such as: "Wow, I'm really inspired. I'm going to sit through the nights!" And that may keep you going, for a period or two. Around three or four in the morning it can get pretty fuzzy, however, and you may find the following much more convincing: "Well, he also said that it's not just about sitting through the nights…" In short, you find yourself swayed by momentary waves of discursive thought. And if you're going on sheer willpower, they will sound very persuasive indeed. Mere willpower is utterly useless here, quite powerless.

Don't give in to what are merely momentary inclinations. If you do, you won't be able to do anything completely, certainly not sustained Buddhist meditation. As your sitting becomes settled, such passing fancies cease to be a problem. This is not mere willpower, but a much more basic kind of dedication. In a word, right effort coming to fruition. Confirm it yourself during this retreat. Right effort allows us to keep the practice constant, without being swayed by such passing fancies.

Don't replace one set of delusions with another. For example, don't waste time and energy using willpower to endlessly cut off thoughts as they arise. You can already see why, can't you? The very effort to stop thoughts arising or to cut them off once they have arisen is itself a kind of willful thought. Wrong effort – striving to put a stop to thought – merely arouses more thoughts, an endless cycle of attacking thoughts with more thoughts. Thus Buddhism emphasizes uprooting the root-source of delusion, rather than endlessly cutting off one blade of grass, then another, and then another. More to the point, the root itself dissolves of its own accord. That is right effort.

Practically speaking, each one of us needs to practice in a way that is appropriate for where we actually are. You may have read books about all kinds of marvelous states and attainments. But if you can't even sit in sustained zazen, if you can't gather all of your energy into the concentrated oneness of samadhi, then you're likely sitting there dreaming up delusions.

Where are you in your actual moment-to-moment practice? Not where do you want to be or where do you think you should be. Then find the practice that is appropriate. One of the reasons we have one-on-one is so that we can go through this together. Then you can clearly see where you actually are, and we can find the practice appropriate for you. This is also a part of right effort.

See what wrong effort is? Endlessly replacing one set of delusions, one form of *dis-ease*, with another. And then another. And then another. Then you wonder why your practice is so tiring, so boring. As the four noble truths make clear, far from the practice of right effort, this is itself a symptom – and a cause – of the continuing *dis-ease*.

Discursive thought endlessly replaces one delusion with another; it may go in many different directions, but it is all wrong effort. *Dis-ease* will never end that way. Let it all go. Do you see? It is the result of *dis-eased* mind endlessly flip-flopping, hip-hopping from one delusion to the next. It has nothing to do with Zen practice.

What is right effort? Being fully engaged in what is right here and now – without discursive thought arising, without fabrication or contrivance of any kind. In other words, directly seeing through the present experience, whether it is one of intense pain or sublime bliss. This is the practice of right effort. It is also the source of true creativity and of compassionate action in the world, whether we are a gardener, a musician, or whatever. Thus we can truly help another in pain by helping them to see through it. Confirm this through your own practice here at this retreat, and in the rest of your life. Find out your self. See through your self.

A formal koan in Zen Buddhism can serve to gather and focus all into one. However, it is not necessary. What is necessary? To see through self. That is really the only koan there is. If you are using a koan and you are not doing that, then face it, you are not really working on a koan. Nor do you need a formal koan in order to do this.

Through right effort, naturally and patiently pour yourself into your practice. Consumed with the practice, there is no room for thoughts of getting closer to – or farther from – some imagined goal. Any such notions are themselves wrong effort.

The practice of right effort reveals this to us.

Beware of thinking that you understand Zen Buddhism. It's really very simple, yet it can be easily misunderstood. Which is why I began by expressing it as, "Can you, by exerting effort, come to rest?" Self is already stuck, entangled in the self-contradiction that it is. Proper practice is not really difficult. But there is something subtle about it that can easily be missed or misconstrued.

The difficulty lies in self's inability to truly see what is. Due to the inherent *dis-ease* that it is, self distorts things through its own lens into something that it can then acquire if it desires, or eliminate if it doesn't. Confronted with the challenge to simply see – and be – what actually is, self is totally at a loss. Thus it concocts some enlightened state that it assumes will solve all its problems, and then strives to achieve it. Or, to conceal its *dis-ease*, self deludes itself into thinking that its confusion is clarity, that it's okay when it's not.

A natural koan can emerge the moment I face the fact that, despite all these charades, self cannot even sustain itself! Right effort, very simply, begins by letting go of all such wrong efforts. Then practice can go smoothly, though it will take time. Patience is a virtue.

Precisely why we have a retreat like this. It is a great inspiration for patient and sustained practice with like-minded folks. Make good use of it.

I have been speaking about thirty minutes. Please feel free to stand up and stretch for a moment. That too is right effort. *[Short break]*

Linji, the outstanding Chinese monk of the Tang Dynasty known in Japanese as Rinzai, is considered the father of Rinzai Zen. One of his renowned sayings is: "The Buddha's teachings are so much toilet paper to wipe your butt with." [See *RL* 19; also see 31, 169-70, and 223.] Does this mean that the sutras and other Buddhist texts are utterly worthless?

Not at all. Once again, Rinzai said that Buddha's teachings are toilet paper to wipe your butt with. See how easy it is – with such an apparently clear-cut metaphor and without sufficient practice or experience – to conclude that therefore such things are utterly worthless?

Did you ever go to the toilet and do your thing, then realize there's no toilet paper? Toilet paper has its place. Everything has its place. It is not worthless by any means. The point Rinzai is boldly declaring has to do with mistaking those precious teachings for the living fact itself.

As I said before the break, be careful thinking that you understand Zen Buddhism. Many of these sayings can be easily misunderstood, even distorted for self-serving purposes. If you are going to take up such Zen expressions you must make them your own, digest them thoroughly – then they can be eliminated.

Rinzai himself said, "I started out devoting myself to the *Vinaya* (monastic code) and also delved into the sutras and *sastras* (commentaries)." [*RL* 21 rev.] By his own admission, he studied these things deeply. He goes on to say, however, that he eventually realized they were prescriptions for salvation. [*RL* 21, 52] What about this?

106

Ever rush to the pharmacy in dire need of medicine – but forget the prescription? Indeed, the prescription has its place. It is not worthless. Again, Rinzai is warning us that the precious prescription is not the medicine itself. No matter how valuable the written word or document, if we do not follow the instructions and faithfully take the medicine, then it really is worthless, isn't it?

Rinzai himself, after carefully studying the words and grasping the prescription, goes on to say how he then threw himself into a Zen monastery. He concludes, "...after exhaustive search and grinding practice, then in an instant I knew my self." [*RL* 21-22 rev.; see also 32.] That is what we are doing here: the natural fruition of right effort.

According to one of those classic Buddhist "prescriptions," Gotama (Sanskrit: Gautama) Buddha, sitting under the Bodhi tree prior to his great awakening, vowed to himself something like, "Flesh, blood, and marrow may dry up in my body, but without complete awakening I will not budge from this seat." [See *LB* 71.] That is right effort. Do you see?

He is not saying you can never take a break – even Gotama had to go to the toilet. The real significance of that statement is revealed when we sit so intently that it is not possible to end our practice – whether we get up, take a nap or whatever. During this retreat we naturally have time for nutritious meals and time to rest. Done properly, these are themselves the practice of right effort, done without budging from our Bodhi seat.

"Flesh, blood, and marrow may dry up in my body, but without complete awakening I will not budge from this seat." Whether Gotama actually said anything like this or not is a concern for historians. Actually come to the end of *dis-ease* – then it is an indisputable fact.

If this is not yet clear, don't worry. Simply give yourself to the practice during this retreat and you will see your self. All you need is to see through now. As Rinzai put it: "Outside this mind there is no Dharma-truth – nor is there anything to be attained within." [*RL* 17 rev.] That is right effort.

Thank you for listening so intently.

THE SUMMIT:
Clearing the Way

(from lectures during the retreat)

Second Day

Two days ago I had the pleasure of taking five Dutchmen, who flew in for this retreat, into center city Philadelphia to visit some historical sights, including the Liberty Bell. On the Liberty Bell is inscribed words adapted from Leviticus 25:10: "...*proclaim liberty throughout all the land unto all the inhabitants thereof...*" Sort of a

Bodhisattva Vow from early Pennsylvania. Pennsylvania was founded as a kind of experiment in religious liberty by William Penn, one of the early members of the Society of Friends, popularly known as Quakers. Many suffered religious persecution, which is one reason they came here.

Over 350 years ago in 1652 the founder of the Society of Friends, George Fox, was wandering in Lancashire in northwest England, where he happened upon a hill. Climbing to the top, there he had the decisive religious experience of his life. He later described it as a vision directing him not to simply obey doctrine and rule but instead to focus upon the inner light – the ability of every person to directly perceive truth. The affinity with Buddhism is obvious. He also described it as a religious truth deriving from immediate perception, although some of the aspects become lost in dogma and doctrine. Again, an obvious affinity with the "Zen doctrine" of not relying on words and letters, of an independent transmission apart from any teaching.

The hill in Lancashire upon which George Fox had this religious experience was called Pendle Hill. Which is why the place where we are now sitting outside of Philadelphia has the same name; this major retreat center of the Society of Friends in the United States was named in its honor. During this retreat, together we will ascend that hill and see for ourselves.

The following traditional Zen koan can help us clear the way. It may not make sense this first telling, but by the end of the retreat it will. It is case 23 of *The Blue Cliff Record* [See *BCR*]: Once a Chinese monk, let's call him Jack, was wandering in the mountains with his fellow monk, let's call her Jill. Jack points and exclaims: "Right here is the summit of mystic peak." Jill responds: "Indeed it is; what a pity." Later this brief exchange was made known to another monk. He said, "If it wasn't for Jill, you'd see skulls covering the fields." What are they talking about? Perhaps this sounds bizarre to you now, like a conversation in a secret language. By the end of the retreat you will see that it is a familiar and natural way for them to speak – though there is no need for us to imitate it.

Today let us focus on the first part. No need to worry about the names of the Chinese monks. For ease of understanding, I inserted familiar names of Jack and Jill. But better yet, let's say it's you. So, YOU are now wandering in the mountains. Intent on religious practice, you have reached the summit.

Right here is our first task: let go of everything and actually ascend the summit where there is nowhere further to go. On the way up it may not be clear at all, it may be very confusing at times. But once we have actually reached the summit, the vista is crystal clear on all sides, without the least vagueness. Having clearly seen, now you must express it: What is it?

"Right here is the summit of mystic peak!" This is the first part of the case as a koan. There is only one way for you to really know this truth. And that is for you to actually be there yourself. Then express what you have seen. The point here is not what someone somewhere long ago meant when he said such-and-such. Is Mystic Peak an actual place of pilgrimage in China or a legendary place in a Mahayana sutra? Or, if we call it Pendle Hill, is it the one in northwest England or the one here in the Philadelphia area? None of these is being addressed here; it is your summit, where you can go no farther, no deeper, no higher.

Again, the first task at this retreat is for each one of us, patiently, calmly, and with right effort to actually arrive here. Clearly, decisively, definitively – not glimpsed through binoculars. Whether you are giving yourself completely to concentrated zazen or working with a koan, it all comes down to this.

These apparently strange koan cases are here to help us on our way. There are many of them. They all point out and express the living truth, yet they do so from different perspectives, to assure that it is seen and lived in every aspect of our lives. This koan case begins with the basic point of religious practice, challenging us first to actually reach the summit and see for ourselves.

Let me introduce one other koan case. It may help you to illumine one case in light of the other. This is case 29 of *The Blue Cliff Record*: A monk asked the master, "The conflagration at the end of the eon destroys the universe, but is *this* destroyed or not?" By way of background, in ancient Buddhist cosmology, at the end of an eon, all that we know as this world will be consumed in flames and come to an end. Then a new eon would begin. All of this is part of *samsara*, the endless cycle of *dis-ease*. Nothing mysterious here; it was the way Buddhists understood the world. How different is it from someone nowadays seeking to understand our world in terms of Genesis, or for that matter, Darwin?

To rephrase the monk's question: "I have seen that all things of this world are temporary, subject to arising and decay. But what about this one, this true self I have realized – it will not be destroyed like all the rest, will it?" Perhaps this monk had some insight or experience, and now he cherishes it. Not so difficult to understand, is it? Perhaps it was gained as the result of great effort – right or wrong, we don't know, as no details of the monk remain. At any rate, he is asking for all of us: when the world is destroyed, is *this* destroyed or not?

The master's response: "Destroyed!" The published translation, adding English syntax, reads: "It is destroyed." – destroying the force of the Chinese, which consists of only one character with no stated subject or object.

The monk, following what he thinks is the master's logic, persists: "Then does *this* go along with it?" The published translation accurately renders the master's response: "It goes along with it." Allow me to freely render the master's response: "Gone!" This koan illumines a slightly different perspective than the koan of the summit. Is it useful for you here and now?

Like the case of the summit, this case can also be taken as three separate but related koans. Today let me just touch on the first koan: A monk asks, "When the world comes to an end, is *this* destroyed or not?" How different is this from the opening koan of the summit? "Right here is the summit of mystic peak!"

To see into these koans, it is helpful to know something of the Buddhist culture from which they naturally derive. And so I have explained something of the background.

But the essential point is to pull the koan out of your self. Or rather, pull your self out of the koan. Otherwise it's just a story about someone else. To be a living koan it must become our own immediate, inevitable question. Thus, in our own practice at this retreat we must actually reach the summit, then we know and can express it: What does it look like? What do you see?

In the second case, if you have realized something – call it this precious one – can it be destroyed? Again, not just these two koans, but every koan is concerned with seeing through self: first of all what I call my self, but also the self of every thing. No need to be preoccupied with the details, the personages and so on of the koan cases. As the great Japanese Zen master Bankei put it, don't get stuck in another man's tub! [See *UB* 133.]

These koan cases have been devised to help us realize no-self – for no-self to realize itself: "Right here is the summit of mystic peak!" Or: "Is *this* destroyed?" Here and now, does anyone have their own living koan to bring forth? *[Pause]*

If not, then continue on into your own. If these two koan cases can serve as grist for the mill, can spur or inspire you, fine. If not, throw them away, or use them as toilet paper. Thank you for listening so intently.

Third Day

I trust you have confirmed for yourself some of the things I have said. For some of you, pain has become a problem. Sitting many, many hours each day in zazen, naturally there is some pain. We are not trying to hurt, of course. That's why it is important to learn to sit properly. Everyone has a different body, so we must learn this for ourselves. We learn by doing it, although yoga stretches and so forth can be helpful to limber up.

Even if you sit well, there will likely be some pain. *Standing* for ten or fifteen hours a day can be painful; confined to a bed for a long time, people develop bedsores. Again, learn to sit properly so as to eliminate or at least minimize the pain. We are not trying to have pain, of course; but neither are we trying to avoid the inevitable pain that we do have. If you have pain, be aware of it. It is your body telling you something – listen.

As your zazen becomes firmly established, you simply *are* the pain; you don't avoid or deny it. Neither do you *react* against it, which causes it to tense up and become worse. For example, when your left knee hurts, you may try to compensate by moving. This usually works – for about a minute or so. Then what happens? It starts to hurt somewhere else. Then you move again. This is not zazen at all, but the physical manifestation of *dis-ease*, restlessness playing hide and seek with itself.

Instead, *be* the pain. If that is your present experience, let it be your koan of the present moment. If it is there, be it. Then to a great extent the pressure can be relieved rather than worsened. It's no miracle, but this can greatly reduce rather than aggravate the pain. It also allows you to continue the constant practice of right effort by *being* what is actually present at the moment.

Tiredness and sleepiness can also be problems. We've sat through two nights so far. Established in the constant practice of right effort, it's not hard to sit through the nights. The samadhi or concentrated oneness is so deep and settled that even when rising from the seat, samadhi gets up and does what must be done. Sustained sitting in deep samadhi is more restful than sleep – certainly more restful than fitful sleep.

If you're not sitting properly, it is difficult to sit through the nights because your sitting causes extra strain. See for yourself: once your sitting is settled, there is nothing more restful. On the other hand, we've all gone to sleep on occasion and woke up feeling worse than when we went to bed! Sleep is not always restful. Awake or asleep, self fills itself with delusions and dreams, worries and nightmares. Sitting through the nights is a fine way to confirm that your sitting is, indeed, settled and that you are becoming established in the constant practice of right effort.

Sitting through the nights, getting hit with a stick – Rinzai Zen has a reputation for severity. And there is some truth to that, especially in a Rinzai monastery. But don't mistake that severity for lack of compassion. Zen Buddhism does not show its compassion in the beautiful manner that some other branches of Buddhism do. But I can assure you, that stick *is* compassion. Here you're not being hit as punishment; you're only being hit when you ask for it, and then to help you in your practice. It can relieve stiff shoulders, wake you up and spur you on. It is even called the stick of compassion.

Likewise, silence can be cold, indifferent. The silence at this retreat is not. Although we are keeping noble silence, if we happen to meet others on the grounds here, we are happy to hear their talk and laughter. It is not a hindrance at all to our silence. Our silence embraces the whole cacophony of marvelous sounds around us. Talk is not always compassionate communication – words can be used as weapons, or to conceal truth. Done properly, our silence, our stillness, even our "severity," is compassion.

Yesterday we took up the first part of the koan case: "Right here *[striking the floor]* is the summit of mystic peak!" I trust this first task is clear – for each one of you to confirm it for yourself. Clearly and without doubt: "Yes, this is it!"

However, the case does not end here. In a sense it *begins* here. Our good friend on the Way cannot help but bow in agreement: "Indeed it is…" Yes indeed, right here is the summit. But then she adds: "…what a pity." Why does she say this? Where does this come from? Here is the second koan of the case.

Once you have truly arrived at the summit, the next step should be obvious. However, as a matter of fact, often it is not. We become blinded by what we have seen. Thus our good friend on the Way kindly pushes us off our high horse.

You may think that the first monk was ignorant and the second monk enlightened. But, at least according to the Zen tradition, both of these monks were speaking from the same place and they understood each other perfectly. They were testing and teasing each other in the utmost seriousness of Zen play. Thus, this "story" continues to inspire us over a thousand years later.

Again, you may think that the summit was lost because the first monk spoke of it; he turned it into "right here." But if it's really living, it can't be lost or lessened, however much we speak of it. Both of them fully and eloquently expressed the truth. "Right here is the summit of mystic peak" is a marvelous and essential spiritual fact. Not only Zen but the Pali texts of early Buddhism make this clear time and again with statements attributed not only to Gotama but to disciples, male and female: with awakening one *realizes* that what must be done has been done, that final freedom has been won, that *dis-ease* has come to an end once and for all, that there is no more becoming, and so on. Needless to say, this is an essential "highlight" on the Path. And we must realize it ourselves.

If it is thoroughgoing, however, right there the second statement inevitably arises, like the valley's echo from a mountaintop cry. From out of the bottomless depths of that summit, the echo comes forth loud and clear: "You're damn right; and ain't that a shame!" In other words, where do you go from there? What do you do with it?

Without first reaching the summit, the resounding echo cannot come forth. But once we have reached the summit, our practice naturally takes a turn. As I mentioned in the beginning, we must practice appropriate for where we actually are on the Way. Where are you? We have just examined the second koan of this case; tomorrow we will see into the third.

We also looked into the case where the monk asks: "When the world comes to an end, is *this* destroyed or not?" Well, maybe all things must pass – but not this! The response: "Destroyed!" With this unequivocal utterance, every last foothold and hiding place is wiped away. Is this the same or different than the koan of the summit? According to Zen tradition, the monk in this case did not get it. What about you?

Fourth Day

We left Jack and Jill up there blabbering on about the summit of mystic peak and what a pity it was. Now for the third and final koan of this case. Later someone else added the comment: "If not for Jill, you'd see skulls covering the fields." What about this? Is something being added, or taken away? Is something clarified, or gone beyond? Without making the koan our own, we cannot get inside. In effect, he is saying that without Jill's precious statement, it would have been dead long ago. How does it continue today as the living, breathing reality that it is? Only YOU can answer that question; and only then can it truly be the living reality that it is.

"Right here is the summit of mystic peak!" First you must arrive here. Then, inevitably arises: "Indeed it is; what a pity." Then a further statement is made – but from where? From the standpoint of lowly delusion? Exalted enlightenment? Finally, where do you stand?

We also looked into the first two koans from the following case. A monk asks: "When the world comes to an end, is *this* destroyed or not?" The master responds: "Destroyed!" Now for the third and final part of this case: The monk, not understanding, persists: "Then does *this* go along with it?" Can you hear the monk tripping over his own feet? This precious one that I have realized, polished and perfected for years – gone, just like all the rest? Seems the monk doesn't want it to be this way. Perhaps he was holding on to some true self which he thought must be unborn, undying, and so on. What about you? On the surface, the master appears merciless, but he is really most merciful. He adroitly responds: "Gone!" Can you go along with that?

These two koans of "the summit of mystic peak" and "destroyed" are not identical. But both in their own way are pointing out, indeed, eloquently expressing, living truth. How do you see it? How do you express it? Baisao was a Zen-tea man living in Kyoto a few hundred years ago; when he got old he committed some of his precious tea utensils to the flames with a poem to the effect:

> *After the eon-ending fire consumes all things*
> *Won't the emerald mountain peak still soar into white clouds?*
> [See *OTS* 84]

We still have several hours; please do not waste this precious opportunity. What remains?

Closing

We are now coming to the completion of our retreat. Thank you to everyone for your precious support. We have been sitting long and hard, giving ourselves fully to our practice.

Be careful that the retreat does not become something that you did, some "peak experience" that you had. Don't turn it into the summit at Pendle Hill. During the retreat you may drop the division that self is. Without the constant practice of right effort, however, once you "return to the world," you may find new divisions arising. With right effort our practice really is seamless; there is no separation – whatever we smack up against. *This* – call it what you like – can it be burned, destroyed, perfected or corrupted?

One special concern now is how to return to the world: to our families, daily lives, and to our work. Wrong effort assures us that when we return we will end up getting in an argument or seeing how everyone else is so utterly unenlightened. With right effort, we pour ourselves fully into our practice at this retreat – a rather special environment. In much the same way, when we return to the world, we pour ourselves into whatever comes next. Just as we have embraced our practice here, we go home and embrace our family, our loved ones. We embrace the joys and pleasures, just as we embrace the challenges and problems.

Let what must be done *be* the practice of the moment. Will it always go smoothly? No. Right there is where our blind spot is revealed. Then we bow, in deep thanks, to the difficulties and challenges as our precious teacher clearing the Way. In this way our practice will proceed, wherever we are.

Thank you for listening so intently. Take great care returning home.

Clarifying the Mind of Nirvana

*(Revised version of lectures for a Zen Buddhist retreat at
Lioba Priory, Egmond, the Netherlands, November 2008.)*

Thursday Night

I am glad we were all able to join in the religious service – the compline – this evening here at the cloister in Egmond. Maybe for some of you it was a bit of a surprise: "We are doing a Zen retreat. Why are we attending a Christian service?" Sharing this space for the next couple of days with practicing Catholics, it is natural to share in their practice as well. Whether we are Catholic or not, it is important to make peace with the religious tradition that we grew up in. Many westerners, myself included, when young went running towards the Orient, towards Buddhism, towards Zen. We were also running away from the religious tradition we grew up in. As we idealized the traditions of the far east, we only saw what was wrong with the traditions we grew up in. Some of you have been to the far east and know that there's good and bad in every religious tradition. It is wonderful that we could share a bit in this other tradition tonight and see its great good. I trust it will help you to make peace with, and see the great good in, the religious tradition you grew up in.

In the Catholic tradition it seems there is a compline service for every day of the year. *Compline* – the very word gives the sense of completion. "Completion" here has a spiritual sense, and refers to more than just the end of the day. Let this be a retreat where we really *complete* practice. Not just forever struggling with or working toward, or trying to attain something, but to truly complete the practice. We all made a sacrifice to come to this retreat. Our family, the people we have left behind, and our coworkers also have to make a sacrifice. So I urge you to practice right effort and truly complete the practice, thus to be worthy of this precious opportunity.

What are we doing here? Very simply, in accord with the Zen Buddhist tradition, we are here to end the delusion of self, *to end the self that seeks for an end*, and in that way realize true freedom. We are not here to learn better ways of dealing with interpersonal relationships. Done properly, this practice should lead in that direction; but that is not the purpose. Nor are we trying to view the world in a new way, to take one view of the world – a Christian view, or an atheist view, for example – and replace it with a Buddhist one. In learning and practicing Buddhism that may happen, but that is not the purpose of a retreat. Nor are we here to learn how to handle our thoughts and our emotions. That too may happen, but that is not the purpose of a Zen Buddhist retreat.

We are doing something much simpler than any of that. There are Buddhist expressions that make this clear. For example, "The mind of Nirvana is easy to clarify; the wisdom of discernment [that is, of genuine distinction and difference] is hard to enter. " [See *ZS* 429.] Practicing properly as we are here at this retreat, it is really not so difficult to clarify the mind of Nirvana. But then to work it out in the world can be a great challenge. Especially in the beginning of retreat, we naturally focus *not* on working it out in the world, but rather on making crystal clear, unmistakably clear, what the source of this mind is. Then we can work it out in the world. A retreat is a matter of going to the very bottom, to the very source. Once the retreat is over and you return to your home and your job, you will have plenty of opportunities to work it out in the world and *complete* it in that sense as well. But we shouldn't be preoccupied with those concerns here.

Where we begin: Putting an end to self-entanglements
Illustration from the Lotus Sutra

There is a famous Buddhist sutra called the *Lotus Sutra*, one of the great Mahayana texts. I will use a story from it as a kind of theme for this retreat. I could take up many things to make the point clear, but this story is a very good one for us here and now. In the *Lotus Sutra*, chapter seven, there is a Buddha whose name literally means something like "The Buddha of Penetrating Wisdom," or "The All Knowing Buddha." This all knowing, great wisdom Buddha is seated on the lotus-shaped Wisdom Throne. In other words, the perfect place in which to practice. And he is seated there in perfect mental and physical poise. He is sitting in the full-lotus posture and his mind is completely at rest, completely motionless in body and in mind. The sutra even says he has destroyed "the army of *mara*" – a metaphor for the illusions and delusions we continually get entangled in. So this Buddha of penetrating wisdom has even destroyed all delusion.

I will continue with this story over the next three mornings. Now your present task is to *be* this all-knowing Buddha – no more, no less. We all have our own lotus throne, this ideal situation here, in which to give ourselves fully to practice, to destroy the army of *mara*, to let go of all self-entanglement. That is our first task. Not to think about it, but to actually *be* it – so grounded, so silent and still in body and in mind, that we *are* this Buddha of penetrating wisdom. This is where we begin.

How do we do this? For those who are more or less beginners, the breath is very helpful. Breathe naturally from the belly and just gather all your energy into one. We are not trying to create visions or to realize esoteric truths. A simple way to destroy the army of *mara* is to gather all of the energy that you have into one. You don't need to force anything. Just simply take all the available energy that you have and patiently roll it all into one. Most of the beginning work is right there, giving one's self fully to the breath in seated zazen.

If there is something that is really driving you in your practice, then you have what could be called a natural koan or a *genjô-kôan*, the koan at hand, the koan manifest here and now. The koan can serve as a kind of anchor for gathering all that available energy into one and keeping it focused. Whether you call it a koan or not doesn't matter. Gathering all into one – whether it's the sitting itself or some specific doubt or koan that is alive and burning for you – it must become w*hat you are*. If there is no such specific problem-question, fine. The sitting itself is enough. Just give yourself so completely to the sitting that the whole army of *mara* – all delusions, as well as any notion of enlightenment – dissolves.

116

We really don't have to *destroy* our delusions. The sutra uses that metaphor, but it can easily be misunderstood as an act of sheer willpower. It's not that kind of thing. When done properly, it's a perfectly natural and constant activity. Effort is involved, but it's not simply an effort of the will. It's as natural as our breathing, but with a total focus on that one point. All of your energy is right here. Whether it's just the sitting itself or even just the breathing itself, or some formulated koan, it doesn't matter as long as it is *you*, without remainder.

You will find sometimes mind wanders. That's okay. The point is to be aware of it. In this kind of concentration, it is very easy to be aware of it. As soon as you start to drift, you are aware of it and you simply come back. You don't need to think about it or judge yourself or compare yourself to the person sitting next to you. That's just more of the army of *mara*. Simply return to one. If the mind wanders again, simply, patiently return to one.

See why a koan can be helpful? It keeps you anchored. Being locked in to the koan, so to speak, keeps the mind from wandering. There's the need to really know, the need to get to the bottom, to see through the koan. A real koan, one that is alive and burning in you, can be a great anchor in your practice. Not an anchor for mere willpower, since with the will you are still on the outside trying to push in. Proper koan practice is a much more subtle and powerful thing than mere willpower. It's not ego-self trying to push in, but rather reality bursting out. That's why you're able to sit through the night – you're so engaged in this, that it is hardly possible to do anything else. It is impossible to go to sleep because you have yet to get to the bottom of it. So you are naturally driven – again, not by mere willpower but a much more fundamental dedication – to get to the very bottom. Some degree of determination is important, but you don't need to push in a willful way. You have already made the commitment to be here and have entered the practice. Now the focus is on right, or proper, effort. Instead of self willfully pushing in from the outside, self gets out of the way. Getting out of the way defeats the army of *mara*. This is our first task: to actually sit through and realize this.

The *Lotus Sutra* speaks of the army of *mara*. Let me speak of the navy: John Paul Jones is considered the father of the American Navy. He was a legendary naval hero during the American Revolution. He was a very determined man. One of his most famous fights was against a vastly stronger, more heavily armed British vessel. They were fighting in the sea off of England when, among other problems, some of the canons on John Paul Jones's ship blew up, killing some of his crew, and setting the ship on fire. The British vessel was very strong and continued to shower the burning ship with canon fire. John Paul Jones's ship was virtually out of control, burning, and so badly damaged that it was sinking.

Do you know what John Paul Jones did at this point? As his ship is sinking and burning he crashes it into the British ship, locking onto it in such a way that it can't get free. The British commander, assuming John Paul Jones is giving up, shouts over to him, "Do you surrender?" His ship is sinking and on fire; what is John Paul Jones's response? According to one account: "Surrender? I have not yet *begun* to fight!"

A few hours later John Paul Jones took command of the British ship, forcing *them* to surrender. So even though John Paul Jones and his crew had almost nothing left, they were so determined that they damaged enough of the British ship to force their surrender.

What is point of this story for us here? After all, this is a Buddhist retreat, and we are doing it in the peace school of a Catholic nunnery! What we need is *not* that fierce, willful determination that allowed John Paul Jones to win the day in a bloody battle. What we need to realize is *that place from which we have not yet begun to fight.* That is where to put forth effort, and where your effort comes from. Do you see? That is where we "fight" from. Then, though we meet various difficulties and challenges, nothing can really get in the way.

In this way, the whole army of *mara* is rendered powerless. Not by attacking it with willful effort, but by allowing mind to return to the original oneness that it is. As long as ego-self remains, then pain, distress, *dis*-ease is inevitable. *Samsara* is inevitable. I trust to some extent you have already realized this – that's why you are here. To repeat: your task here and now is to sit as this Buddha of penetrating wisdom, giving yourself completely to the practice. Then you cannot help but see through *samsara*.

Friday Morning

Sitting through the night I trust you have all tasted for yourself that there is nothing to attain. For the seeking, grasping self there are endless things to attain or to escape from. In a word, that whole complex is *samsara*. It is *samsara*, *dis-ease*, distress, because the self cannot come fully to rest. To some extent you all already know this – and yet you continue to seek, don't you? I trust you have seen directly that there is nothing to attain. Decisively attaining *that* is what Buddhism is about. Not just intellectual knowledge, feeling, or insight, but the actual ending of the self that endlessly seeks.

Though some of you have already realized this to some extent, your seeking mind continues to function, and you are aware of this. There is nothing to attain, and yet this urge, this *samsaric* condition, the self's *dis*-ease, is still functioning. So a delicate but very important part of practice is to see that and to allow it to come to rest, to come to its own end – without remainder.

> *Self-entanglements at an end, yet no awakening*
> *Zazen as clarifying, not denying, the doubt you are*
> *Theme from the Lotus Sutra Continued*

Do you see? Your own experience is similar to that of the Buddha in the *Lotus Sutra* mentioned last night. This Buddha of penetrating wisdom sat perfectly on his lotus throne not just for a couple of days, but for endless kalpas. And yet, to continue the story from the sutra, *he did not awaken.* It wasn't that he failed to sit long enough or well enough. The sutra is clear: This Buddha of penetrating wisdom sat *perfectly* on the lotus seat; in other words, in all the right conditions – full lotus, completely at rest in body and mind – for endless kalpas! Yet, the sutra goes on to say, "Seated on that lotus throne, having destroyed the armies of *mara*, this Buddha of Penetrating Wisdom was just about to attain perfect and complete enlightenment, but the Buddha Dharma was not revealed to him."

What about this? Is this perhaps your situation? Are you sitting the best that you can on your lotus throne, attaining profound and subtle states of mind in the process? Do you see what the sutra is saying? This Buddha got all the conditions right: posture and mind flawless, army of delusions wiped out – for an endless period of time. And yet the Buddha Dharma was not revealed to him. He did not awaken. What about this? What about you? Is this in some sense your question, your situation, your doubt? If not, what is?

In Zen there are expressions like, "Get the question clear and you're close to an answer!" Get your question – the real question, the doubt that you are – clear. Do not just sit there in a state of deep samadhi or concentrated oneness, but *be perfectly clear*. Is there something lacking? Is there some question, some doubt? If there is, make it perfectly clear. Why? Because that's the way to the real solution. Make the question or doubt – what is lacking in you – crystal clear. Then the "answer" or "solution" – *the collapse of the self that is stuck* – is inevitable.

To use a dramatic Zen metaphor, "With bow broken and arrows exhausted, *there* shoot with your whole being." [See *ZCM* 30.] That's what we do in zazen; that's what we do with a koan. See why this kind of extremity is necessary? As long as self maintains its delusion, has one more arrow left in its quiver, one more thing it can do, it will do it. It will keep chasing its tail. Deep inside you know it doesn't work, you know it doesn't strike the heart of the matter, but you don't know what else to do. Proper zazen is a very effective way to let all of that habit energy just dissolve. And then, as I said last night, with all available energy gathered into one – with bow broken and arrows exhausted – *there* the balloon of self is punctured once and for all.

Without this extremity, the self will just continue making itself bigger, or smaller, attempting to "make a difference." Due to its inveterate *dis-ease*, self wants to make a difference, to change things somehow. But it only ends up expanding or contracting the delusive circle it is running around in. Face it: self wants to improve the situation, to make a difference – but self can't really make a difference. That "difference" is the delusion that self maintains in order to maintain itself. That is *samsara*.

Of course, I urge you after the retreat to go back to the world – your family, your work, your loved ones, your enemies if you have any – and work this out and in that sense "make a real difference." But that is not our work here in retreat. Our work here is first to make crystal clear that there is no way for self to make a difference. In the religious world, in entering Zen, every "way" must finally be done away with. Otherwise it can get in the way, can become an obstacle. Yes, even zazen. In the depths of your zazen here and now – however deep it is – *there cannot even be a hint of zazen*, let alone some kind of illusion to eliminate or enlightenment to attain. To some extent you have all tasted this already. It's not something out there, it's what you are at bottom, right here and right now.

Right effort is not an effort of the will

Now, what about this Buddha of penetrating wisdom? What about you? We have a little less than two days left, but that is kalpas if we use it well. Sit zazen until nothing remains. Sit until there is *nothing* left. Sit until there *is* nothing to attain.

Do you see why I use that statement of John Paul Jones? – "I have not yet begun to fight!" He was expressing a very willful determination, but that's not what we're doing here. Rather, we are realizing *that which has not yet begun to fight*. That which is not divided into two, the inseparable, the indivisible – then working from there.

When Gotama Buddha was sitting under the Bodhi tree, his lotus seat, according to Chinese accounts he said to himself something like, "Skin, flesh, and marrow may dry up in my body, but without complete awakening I will not move from this seat." This is easy to misunderstand. Like John Paul Jones, this seems to be expressing a tremendous effort of the will. But it's not that kind of thing at all. Gotama Buddha got up sometimes, for example, to relieve himself. It's not a matter of gritting your teeth and stubbornly refusing to budge. It doesn't mean that you can't get up from this posture. It means that even when you *do* get up and break the posture to go for a meal, for a walk or a rest, you do not stop your practice. *That's* the sort of determination or effort he is expressing. Not mere willpower. Willful effort was what Gotama came to the limits of at the end of his arduous ascetic practices, prior to sitting under the Bodhi tree. When he realized he was not getting enlightened but instead was killing himself, he decided to refresh himself, take nourishment and bathe in the river. Then he sat down and said, "Skin, flesh, and marrow may dry up in my body, but without complete awakening I will not move from this seat." This is much more basic than mere willful effort. It's the commitment that from now on, whatever I do, I will not budge from this seat. I *cannot* budge from this seat. Then the lotus seat is where we are, wherever we are and whatever we do. It's not a matter of just sitting in a certain posture and being very stubborn.

Does anyone have a question from out of their practice that they want to raise for everyone, instead of in one-on-one?

Questioner: I have a question about effort. I find myself sometimes using my will, and find that the very use of will becomes the obstacle. So then I try just sitting here, yet sometimes that seems a bit like twiddling my thumbs. So then I try to barrel-ass through with my will, which again becomes an obstacle. So I keep struggling with my own failures.

Jeff: There is a place for determination and will. You would not be here if you didn't have determination. You've all made plans and preparations to come here, and now you're dealing with your passing fancies and momentary inclinations – all those great experiences you dreamt of having when you came here, as you struggle to stay awake. Yes, there is a place for determination. If we simply sit here twiddling our thumbs, that will not do. The problem is when it becomes wrong effort, the will trying to will itself into enlightenment, to pull itself up by its own bootstraps. The very effort maintains the delusion. Or you try to focus and you find your mind wandering. Instead of simply bringing it back, you find yourself engaged in a dialogue with yourself about your mind having wandered. This is just continuing that whole process of your mind wandering, isn't it? You don't have to be happy about your mind wandering, but you don't have to get angry either. Just simply bring it back. And that is a kind of effort, a kind of determination.

Right effort is not mere willpower though. Nor is it, as you suggest, simply sitting there twiddling your thumbs. That's going backwards instead of forwards – the point is to stop! So you're quite right. It will not do to simply barrel-ass through with will. But it will not do simply to say to hell with it, I'll just sit here, stay relaxed, and not try too hard. You've already seen that neither of those will do.

For you here and now, right effort is sitting – as Gotama Buddha did – with the resolve not to get up until you have gotten to the end of yourself. It doesn't mean you don't get up from your cushion. It means the resolve to continue on this path until the end *no matter what, in whatever you are doing.* This means maintaining your practice when you are confused and frustrated too. If you are confused, recognize it. That is your practice at the moment. If that's where you are, be there, even though it may not be pleasant. If you're confused, be a confused Buddha. But don't be confused about your confusion. Nor is it a matter of simply giving up on effort altogether and not trying. It's a matter of putting effort in the right place, so to speak. It's not going outward, but it's not really going inward either. It's seeing through where that division arises from. Right there. And it's always right here and right now. It's not something we will attain some day as the result of some superhuman effort. This – pain in the legs right now – *is* the mind of Nirvana, if we actually see through it. It's unmistakable. No one can take that away from you; no one can give it to you either. From there, the very struggle and distress that you speak of is transformed into the Way itself.

Questioner: My experience is that it's something that comes from out of the blue, and not something I can engineer.

Jeff: No one has awakened in the Zen tradition simply sitting in meditation. Look at the records. According to the Zen tradition, even Gotama Buddha – though sitting in meditation – awakened upon looking up and seeing the morning star. He wasn't just meditating. You'll never get there *by* meditating. Not to say that zazen is useless, of course. Not at all. That's like saying, "Even if I plow the field and plant the seeds, that's not the food." Well, that's right. But if you don't put the seeds in and plow the field, and take care with the water, you won't have the conditions you need for food. So even though there's not a direct cause-effect relationship – I sit, and then I get enlightened – *conditionally speaking,* awakening does take conditions.

No, awakening cannot simply be engineered; but practice should be done with right effort. In other words, we don't practice in order to get something. We do it so purely and wholeheartedly that there can be no room for "Am I going to get it? Am I closer?" That very thought is wrong effort. Give yourself so completely to practice that there can be no room for such things.

As Dôgen himself admits, he wasn't just sitting in meditation when he awakened. During early morning zazen, the monk next to him fell asleep. Seeing this, the master shouted, "Zazen is the practice of body-mind dropped off – how can you sit there sleeping?!" And with that, for Dogen – not for the dozing monk – body-mind dropped off. In other words, "body-mind" or everything that one can identify as one's self, was "dropped off," in other words, gone. Period. But simply sitting cannot *cause* this.

Do you see what this has to do with the Buddha of penetrating wisdom? He did it all, for kalpas – forever! You'll never do that. And yet he didn't attain it. Skating on thin ice, you're right where that Buddha is! Right here it becomes even more important to practice properly, which includes doing it without any purpose at all. If you have any intent to become a Buddha, engineered or not, your practice is not yet pure. Do you see? Precisely because it can't be contrived, it can't be engineered, you don't *stop* sitting. On the contrary, you sit *completely*.

Thank you for your questions and comments. To some extent, everyone is struggling with the same concerns, so your questions are helpful for all. Thank you all for listening so intently.

Saturday Morning

> *Sitting perfectly, yet failing to awaken*
> *A Zen koan: Confronting the aspiration to attain awakening*
> *Completing the story from the Lotus Sutra*

Let me return now to that story from the *Lotus Sutra*: the Buddha of penetrating wisdom was sitting on the lotus throne for eons, perfectly at rest in body and mind, and yet Buddhahood was not revealed to him. This actually became a kind of great doubt for at least one Chinese Zen monk long after the sutra was written. Perhaps like you, this monk couldn't swallow it. So, according to case nine of *Gateless Barrier*, he asked the master about it. He was not only asking about this legendary Buddha of an infinite past who practiced for millions of years. He was asking about his own practice: "It says that the Buddha of All-knowing Wisdom sat zazen on a Bodhi seat for kalpas. Yet the Buddha Dharma was not manifested, nor did he attain Buddhahood. Why?" Not a bad question, is it? What do you think the master says in response? What do you say? "Why?"

The master responded, "That's a marvelous question." In Chinese this kind of response is called chasing after the robber on his own horse. Some masters might strike the monk, "Fool, don't ask such stupid questions!" But this master, at that time and place, responded what a marvelous question it was. He doesn't deny where the monk is coming from at all. Instead he embraces the monk to help him see through. Do you see where the master is coming from when he says what a fine question it was?

But the monk doesn't get it. So he persists. Perhaps he has put in a lot of time and feels it is all wasted now. So he again says, "He sat zazen on a Bodhi seat. Why did he not attain Buddhahood?!" The monk persisted. He did not give in to the master. How does the master respond? How do you respond? How do we really help that monk here?

The master responded, "Because he didn't attain Buddhahood." It doesn't record that the monk was enlightened with that response. But it was taken as such a precious exchange between monk and master that it has continued down to this day for over a thousand years.

Is this your own living, vital question? If not, what is? "I've put in a great deal of time and effort, struggled with a lot of pain and sleepiness. Where am I now?" Good question. Where are you now? Again, get the question clear and you're close to the answer. If you get the question clear and precise, you're right on top of the answer. You can't miss it. The question will drive you there. The question – or if you don't have a question, the sitting itself – becomes you, then caves in on itself. You *become* the question, the sitting itself. And with that, self-delusion ends. It cannot be maintained. It is "un-selfsustainable." It is only the machinations of the deluded self that keeps some semblance alive.

The master said to the monk, "What a marvelous question." To rephrase it, "Take that question all the way and you're there!" Thus, when asked again, the master very kindly responded, "Because he did not attain Buddhahood." He doesn't give the monk anything – or take anything away. No excuses. No explanations. No consolation. Not even criticism. Nothing. *See through right there!* Don't give me analyses or descriptions. Simply see through the question itself. Really see through it, then there can be no doubt: attaining Buddhahood or not doesn't make the least bit of difference!

Questioner: What is the meaning of the word "attain"?

Jeff: To attain is to achieve. In the *Four Great Vows* as commonly recited, the word attain is used: "I vow to attain the Buddha Way." And that's the challenge from the *Lotus Sutra*. For the struggling self, trying to attain something is all it has. But what does it really mean to "attain Buddhahood" – is that not your question? Can self *attain* no-self? The self attempts to use its old bag of tricks here: "I want this; tell me what to do so I can get it." The master's statements here undercut that very delusion.

We cannot bring self-delusions on the Buddha way. It will not work. That is what the monk could not see, what he could not "attain." In a word, to attain *that* is what it's about. And that's not something self can attain; rather it is the end of the whole self-complex. The *Lotus Sutra* makes clear that this Buddha is doing all that he needs to do to attain his goal – all of the practices, the *paramitas*, charity, meditation, and so forth. That's precisely what this koan is asking about. This

Buddha did everything right, but did not attain Buddhahood. Why? Do you see? And that became the sticking point for that monk, so he raised the question: If the all-knowing Buddha can't even attain it, how the hell can I?!

You can't. Real practice begins here, when you realize that self cannot do anything about it. Self cannot attain it. That's the nub of your question. That's why we sit like this – without our little bag of tricks.

In the beginning, self cannot help but chase its own tail; that's all it knows how to do. It seeks a technique to end its suffering – and ends up extending that very suffering in the process. Instead of trying to escape from your situation, what if you took your doubt, your question, all the way? Thus the master kindly leaves the monk with his question. In effect: "That'll do – now take it all the way."

"An ordinary person realizes it and becomes a sage. A sage sees through it and becomes an ordinary person." [See *ZS* 608.] We have to – not attain – but *realize* it, *actualize* it. However we express it, the fact is we don't become superhuman Buddhas. By really being who we are, we realize what it is to be a sage or a Buddha. And really realizing what it is to be a sage is to *be* – and to be content with – the ordinary person we are: no odor of enlightenment, no stench of realization. You see how immature that is, how it cannot be the fruition. It's more like something rotting.

Layman Pang was a Tang dynasty Chinese layperson who was deeply realized. But like most of us, he did not become a monk or priest. Layman Pang says in one of his famous poems something like, "Carrying firewood and hauling water – how marvelous!" He fell through as a layman, and he did it in such a way that it naturally became what he was doing. "Sitting on the Buddha Throne – how marvelous!" But for Layman Pang it was hauling water from the well and carrying firewood. You see? That's the sage becoming an ordinary person – all stink of attainment is gone. This is very important. [See *SLP* XIX, 15.]

Just doing what must be done at that time and place *is* the freedom we seek. But ego-self cannot attain that. It seeks to get away from limitations and responsibility: "I want to be free." Thus it remains shackled to itself. Ego-self cannot really recognize that doing what must be done *is* utter freedom. Complete freedom. Whether we are carrying firewood or answering the telephone. When ego-self is gone, anything will do; and as long as ego-self remains, nothing will do. Thus we practice like this.

Again I ask you, what about the Buddha of penetrating wisdom? What about *you* in your practice? We have one day left; make good use of it.

Sunday Morning

Working it out in the world

One thing that should be touched on now is how to take the practice into our daily lives. All of you have had to struggle – to face yourselves, to struggle with sleepiness, pain, and many other things. But you've all been able to go through and reach some depth – if I may use that expression – in your practice.

Now we take it to the streets. Now we return to our home, family, work, messages that have piled up, and so on. We have given ourselves completely in our practice here sitting on the cushion. Giving ourselves to the breath, to being one, to *mu*. When you go back to your family, your home, give yourself there as well. It's not quite the same thing. You won't be sitting fifteen hours a day – you don't need to. That's what we do *here*. When you go home, please give yourself to what needs to be done there with the same sincerity and dedication that you have given yourself to practicing here. Then there will be no discord between the two. No, it will not be the same; but it won't be completely different either. Thus it remains seamless, without disruption.

Returning home, embrace your loved ones, embrace your family, embrace the work you have to do. Embrace your enemies if you have any. In that way the practice goes smoothly. I am not saying from now on you will have no problems. I *am* saying when you face a problem, face it squarely. Be it. Don't stand on the outside judging, blaming, or trying to escape. Thus we become grateful for those challenges as our precious teacher. Then nothing can get in the way of the practice. Everything becomes grist for the mill, a precious treasure. Everything.

If, on the other hand, you go back and neglect your home and family so you can practice hours of zazen, so you can keep your "retreat high" – you see the problem. That is wrong effort. Go back without disrupting home and family. It's important to apply yourself constantly so there can be no interruption, no gap in the practice. You have seen the value here over the last couple days of constant practice. That continues as you return to the world, but it becomes more complex: "The mind of Nirvana is easy to clarify; the wisdom of discernment is hard to enter." Give yourself to it without a moment's hesitation. *Don't try to hold on to some state you have reached.* Any state you have reached, throw it away. That's not it, so don't worry – you don't need to hold onto it. If there's something that can be lost, let it go now. Gone! Throw it away. In that way our practice continues seamlessly.

I mentioned Layman Pang, who referred to the everyday act of carrying water as "marvelous." What is being expressed here? Doing what must be done at the moment *is* complete and total freedom. When you can give yourself completely, not holding anything back, to what must be done at the moment, *that* is complete freedom. Unhindered, unbound. Whether you're carrying firewood, or checking email – not as romantic sounding, I know. Again, ego-self cannot attain this. Many traditional koans make this clear. Your own practice makes this clear, doesn't it? Ego-self cannot attain this, so it comes to an end. Actually coming to an end, there is nothing whatsoever to attain, within or without. Nor is there anything remaining to go beyond.

Have you seen clearly this Buddha of penetrating wisdom? Have you sat on his lotus throne? Have you clearly seen through your not attaining Buddhahood? This practice is precious indeed. You have all made great sacrifices coming here. But this practice is not the answer to every particular problem. In a profound sense, this practice is also completely useless. You don't get anything out of it. Nothing. That's why it's invaluable. If you think that by doing this practice all your problems will be solved, you've got a big problem indeed! That is using practice to escape from problems. Don't fall into that trap.

When you sit, sit so thoroughly that there is no self sitting. There is not even zazen in this depth of sitting. Then when you get up and respond and work in the world, it's not the same mind, nor a different mind, so it works freely and effortlessly. That doesn't mean we can then solve all the problems of the world. But it's a good place to start – getting self out of the way. It gives us a place to begin to really resolve problems at the root, rather than going in the same old circles. So don't use the practice as an excuse or escape from the actual problems in the world or with others. And when you confront a problem within or without, deal with it directly. Bow in thanks for that challenge or problem and you will see the way through. Thank you.

Afterword

As you have seen from the book in your hands, Jeff Shore's lifework is focused on the practice of Zen. Jeff is a Zen Man and not a Zen priest, not a Zen monk. He completed his Zen training under Keidô Fukushima Roshi (1933-2011), then Zen Master of Tôfuku(ji)-*sôdô* (the training monastery of Tôfukuji) and head abbot of the Tôfukuji branch of Rinzai Zen Buddhism. Fukushima Roshi made Jeff Shore a Dharma heir and put him to the task of teaching westerners, a task which Roshi himself had endeavored throughout his teaching life. Jeff has been quietly traveling the world over, giving intensive training sessions (traditionally called *sesshin*) and one-on-one (traditionally called *dokusan/sanzen)* as well as lecturing on Zen training and living. So what you have in Jeff Shore is a Rinzai Zen Master (the only westerner to complete the training in a Rinzai monastery) who is a householder with a wife and son, and who has a "regular" job. His "regular" job is professor of Zen in the Modern World at Hanazono University in Kyoto, the sole Rinzai Zen University in the world. He is credentialed as they say, but let me offer a brief story so you might get some of the flavor of Jeff's Zen as I experienced it when I first came to know him.

It was in the winter training season at Tôfukuji during a cold snap. For many of us in training the first signs of frostbite had set in and the 4-month runny nose had started to drip. We were all preparing ourselves for the first fifty-minute zazen period of the evening, arranging our robes to wrap up our leg posture and bringing our concentration to bear on our sitting when one of the senior monks enters the monks hall and quietly announces in Japanese to the most senior monk that "Jeff-san is coming." We all get up and rearrange the seating order, bring another set of cushions down from what I like to call the "overheard storage compartment" and get back to our preparation.

As I'm settling into my seat, I hear this swishing sound. I can almost recognize the sound but can't quite place it. "*Zip Zip Zip*" at a kind of walking pace. I see, through the open sliding *shoji* screen, Jeff-san coming down the walk and around the side of the monks hall. The sound is coming from him; he crosses the threshold, bows and makes his way upstream to his seat. As he walks by I get a glimpse of him and his swish sound. He is wearing what are called warm-up pants – sometimes called track pants or trackies. In my neighborhood they were called "swishy" pants because of the sound they made. "Swishy pants?" I thought to myself, "What is this guy thinking?" Of course he was also sporting a dark leather biker vest over his zipper sweater. Again, "What is this guy thinking, wearing a leather vest in a Buddhist monastery, and those noisy-ass swishy pants?" This guy was breaking some serious conventions. He's in a biker jacket while the Japanese laymen who drop in to train usually wear traditional Japanese gear. He takes his seat, brings his legs up into full lotus and prepares himself like he had been doing this for years. Actually it's been several decades, but I didn't know that. Weeks later we snuck a quick meeting and got to talk a bit.

What I found and still find so refreshing in Jeff is his ordinary way. His is ordinary in the sense of being simply at home. I have seen him intense, easygoing, intellectually astute and even curious. He is ordinary in a way that is extraordinary. He brings that "no bullshit ordinary" into his teaching and interactions, and I trust you have found it in this book. Jeff clearly comes out of the living Buddhist tradition. Yet he expresses it in an especially refreshing "no Zen-bullshit" manner. Practical commentaries on traditional poems, koans and Buddhist teachings peppered with Jackson Browne, T. S. Eliot and Meister Eckhart. What I see in Jeff Shore's work, both writing and personally, is the intention to be as direct and connective as possible. There are no esoteric games or exotic conundrums here. Jeff is a very plain pointer and he is deeply committed to you thoroughly seeing through to the very bottom. By now you have gotten a sense of his purpose. *Zen Classics for the Modern World* is a great resource. It is my hope that it may continue to inspire you in your own spiritual life.

Peace.

The Reverend Justin Lanier
St. Patrick's Church
Lebanon, OH, USA

Glossary of Terms

Âsrava
See Outflow.

Bodhisattva
A being who has postponed his or her final enlightenment (and consequent release from *samsara*) in order to save all suffering beings. Originally referring only to previous incarnations of the Buddha (before his attainment of awakening), "Bodhisattva" can also denote any practitioner on the path to Buddhahood.

Buddhahood
The attainment of awakening (the original meaning of "Buddha") and consequent liberation from the *dis-ease* of *samsara*.

Buddha Nature
The innate potential of all sentient beings to awaken and become Buddha.

Dharma
One of the "Three Treasures" of Buddhism, along with the Buddha and the Sangha (the community of practitioners). Dharma refers to the collection of all Buddhist teachings as well as the "living truth" they represent.

Dhyâna
A deep state of meditative absorption (samadhi). Although the word traditionally refers to any of eight increasingly profound concentration states, *dhyâna* may also simply refer to the act of meditation itself. See Paramitas.

Dis-ease
A translation of the Sanskrit word *dukkha*, the first of the Four Noble Truths of Buddhism. The word has often been rendered into English as "suffering," a translation that somewhat distorts the word's meaning. *Dis-ease* is the deep sense of dissatisfaction inherent in being attached to the delusion of a permanent self. Cf. *samsara*.

Eightfold Path
See Noble Truths.

Four Great Vows
Also referred to as the "Bodhisattva Vows," the Four Great Vows are central to the practice of Mahayana Buddhism and are chanted daily in Zen monasteries. They are: 1. Beings are numberless – I vow to save them all. 2. Delusions are endless – I vow to extinguish them all. 3. Dharma gates are boundless – I vow to learn them all. 4. The Buddha Way is supreme – I vow to attain it.

Genjô-kôan
Literally the "manifest koan," this is the religious question that arises naturally

from the heart of one's own *dis-ease*. *Genjô-kôan* also refers to the resolution of that religious question through awakening.

Heart Sutra

Although only a couple pages in length, the *Mahaprajna Paramita Heart Sutra (J. Makahannya Haramita Shingyô)* is a major text in Zen Buddhism. Chanted several times daily in Zen monasteries, this sutra asserts that each and every phenomenon is fundamentally without self and that awakening to this truth puts an end to all *dis-ease*. *Mahaprajna Paramita*, literally "the perfection of great wisdom," is a central concept to the *Prajna Paramita* genre of Buddhist literature, originating in India in the 1st century C.E. The *Mahaprajna Paramita Heart Sutra* is thus named because it is said to contain the essence (heart) of the entire *Prajna Paramita* teaching.

Immediate awakening

Often translated as "sudden enlightenment," this term stands in contrast to "gradual enlightenment," the doctrine that enlightenment is perfected little by little over a long period of time. "Immediate awakening" means that realization is instantaneous and without mediation.

Kalpa

An immensely long period of time, traditionally used in Buddhist texts to illustrate the amount of time required for beings to attain Buddhahood over many lifetimes. One popular way of depicting a kalpa is that it is the time required to wear away a boulder of incalculable immensity, if one were to brush it once every hundred years with a tuft of wool.

Kenshô

Literally, "seeing into the nature." Kenshô is another word for Zen awakening. This should not be confused with samadhi, which is a highly concentrated state of mind. Kenshô is not a state of mind, but rather the realization of emptiness itself, although its use in English today tends to refer to mere glimpses or experiential insights.

Koan

Literally meaning "public case." Koans are usually recorded encounters between Zen masters and their disciples. Often the disciple had a realization through the encounter. Eventually these recorded cases were used to provoke realization in others by focusing on the point of the koan during zazen and in daily life.

Mahayana

Literally "the greater vehicle." The term is used to distinguish this branch of Buddhism from its earlier forms (sometimes disparagingly called Hinayana, the "lesser vehicle"). Mahayana takes as its ideal the Bodhisattva path and thus is concerned with the salvation of all beings, not just individual awakening. Zen is one of many branches of Mahayana Buddhism.

Mara

The "tempter demon" of Buddhist mythology. Mara failed in his efforts to distract Gotama Buddha from his meditation beneath the Bodhi Tree by conjuring up seductive visions of beautiful women.

Mu

Literally, "no/nothing." In Zen, *Mu* is being without self. *Mu* also refers to the first case of the koan collection, *Mumonkan:* "A monk asked the master, 'Does the dog have Buddha nature or not?' The master said, "*Mu!*" [see *ZCM*].

Noble Truths

The Four Noble Truths as expounded by Gotama Buddha. They are 1. Life is *dis-ease*. 2. Blind craving and attachment are the cause of this *dis-ease*. 3. There is liberation from this *dis-ease* through awakening. 4. This is done by following the Eightfold Noble Path of Right Views, Right Intention, Right Speech, Right Action, Right Livelihood, Right Effort, Right Mindfulness, and Right Concentration.

Outflow *[âsrava]*

Originally referring to foam which rises to the top of boiling rice, *âsrava* signifies the proclivity of the mind to become scattered by attending to external objects. In deep zazen, this activity is brought to rest.

Paramitas

The *paramitas* or "perfections" are six virtues that a Bodhisattva practices and perfects along the path to Buddhahood. They are: *dâna* (generosity), *sîla* (precepts), *ksânti* (forbearance), *virya* (unflagging effort), *dhyâna* (meditative absorption), and *prajnâ* (wisdom).

Rinzai Zen

The Rinzai (Chinese: Linji) school is one of two major branches of Japanese Zen. Transmitted to Japan by the monk Myôan Eisai (1141 – 1215) in 1191, Rinzai Zen today is characterized by its use of koans as the focus in zazen. The Rinzai school was inspired by the monk Linji Yixuan (d. 867), known for his harsh and sometimes even violent teaching style. Today, Rinzai lineages in Japan descend from the master Hakuin Ekaku (1686 – 1768).

Samadhi

The concentrated state of becoming one with the object of meditation.

Samsara

Samsara is the ancient Indian view of the world as an endless karmic cycle of death and rebirth owing to delusion. Through awakening, there is liberation from *samsara* and thus no more rebirth.

Sangha
See Dharma.

Shikan-taza
Literally "just sitting." *Shikan-taza* is uncontrived sitting, without an object of meditation. It is the primary practice of Sôtô Zen.

Six senses
In addition to the five senses of sight, hearing, smell, taste, and touch, Buddhism includes consciousness as a sixth sense.

Sôtô Zen
One of the two major branches of Japanese Zen. The Sôtô (Chinese: Caodong) school was transmitted to Japan by the master Dôgen Kigen (1200 – 1253) in 1228. Originally one of the "Five Houses" of Chinese Zen, the Caodong school is named after its founders Dongshan Liangjie (806 – 869) and his disciple Caoshan Benji. Although the Sôtô school has more recently come to practice *shikan-taza* exclusively, in the past it also made use of koans.

Zazen
Literally "seated Zen." Seated meditation practiced in Zen.

Index

I

Immediate awakening 頓悟, 89, 130

J

Jesus, xv, xvi
Jion [see Ziyuan]
Johnson, Samuel, 83
Jones, John Paul, 117–118, 120
Just sitting [see *Shikan-taza*]

K

Kakuan Shion [see Guoan Shiyuan]
Kalpa, 86, 94, 118, 119, 120, 122, 130
Karmic consciousness 識心, 57, 61, 64
Kenshô 見性, vi, viii, 22, 130
Kinhin 経行, iv
Koan 公案, xi, xiii, 48, 50–54, 57, 58, 61, 63, 64, 105, 106, 108–110, 111, 112, 114, 116, 117, 119, 122, 123, 125, 128, 130, 131, 132

L

Lanzan [see Nanyue Mingzan]
Lao-zi (Lao Tzu) 老子, 26
Lay (layman/laywoman/ lay practice), i, vii, 15, 44, 48, 55, 73, 78–80, 82, 127
Lazy Zan [See Nanyue Mingzan]
Layman Pang 龐居士, xii, 124, 125
Lingyun [Zhiqin] 靈雲志勤, 47
Linji [Yixuan] 臨済義玄, 27, 79, 80, 82, 89, 90, 91, 93, 94, 95, 96, 99, 106, 131
Linjilu [see *Record of Linji*]
Lotus Sutra, 116, 117, 118, 122–123
Luohan [Guichen] 羅漢桂琛, 47, 58–59

M

Mahayana [Buddhism] 大乘, xv, xvii, 60, 108, 129, 130
Mara, 116–119, 131
Mazu [Daoyi] 馬祖道一, 49
Merton, Thomas, xv–xvi
Mind of life-and-death 生死心, 66
Ming Dynasty, 47, 57, 79
Mu 無, 15, 19, 125, 131

Mumon [see Wumen]

N

O

P

Q

R

S

"Jeff Shore brings forty years of training and teaching experience in meditative practice and textual studies of Zen Buddhism to bear in his translations and interpretations of three valuable classics about pathways to awakening. Shore's commentaries on these works, combining profound knowledge of a thousand-year old literary tradition with contemporary cultural allusions and fresh insights, are consistently fascinating and illuminating, and in true Zen style, frequently humorous and disarming. Several short essays, included here by those who have trained under him, put in useful perspective just how intriguing and motivating Shore's teaching style is."
— *Steven Heine, Professor and Director of Asian Studies, Florida International University, renowned author, translator, and editor of works on Zen Buddhism*

"A collection of old Zen stories far away from our own lives? Not at all! This book points directly to the core of our own lives and being. To recognize this, it's necessary to read it not just with mind but with heart. Then the words can turn into real guidelines on the Way, on the Way to find out what we really are. You may have long been searching in theories, in books, to find answers to your questions – but have you really come to the end of your quest?
No, this book won't offer pat answers or a quick "fix" for personal problems. Answers can only be found inside yourself. This requires courage, to let the words settle into mind and body, and to let them unfold there. What happens then? Open the book and find out!"
— *Jeannette Stowasser, Munich, Germany*

"Zen Buddhism cannot be learned from a book. Direct personal contact with a genuine Zen teacher is at the heart of the tradition. After over 12 years of experience with Jeff Shore, I can confirm without doubt that he is such a teacher. If you do not have the opportunity to join a retreat and have this personal encounter, the next best thing you can do is to digest this book. And in full accord with the Buddha's teaching, let me add: don't believe me – see for yourself."
— *Stefan van Weers, Zutphen, Netherlands*

"As a Zen practitioner, I am forever grateful to have encountered Jeff Shore along the Way. As a member of Jeff's family through marriage for over thirty years, I have had ample opportunities to observe him in innumerable situations. His commitment – to his own Path as well as tirelessly being there for others – has been unwavering. In this unique volume of translations and retreat lectures, Jeff goes right to the heart of our search for spiritual freedom."
— *Tina Shore, Nurse Psychotherapist, Rockville, Maryland*